JOB SEARCH FOR THE
TECHNICAL
PROFESSIONAL

JOB SEARCH FOR THE TECHNICAL PROFESSIONAL

DAVID J. MOORE

John Wiley & Sons, Inc.

New York • Chichester • Brisbane • Toronto • Singapore

Library of Congress Cataloging-in-Publication Data:

Moore, David J. (David Jewel), 1936–
    Job search for the technical professional / by David Moore.
      p.   cm.
    Includes bibliographical references and index.
    ISBN: 0-471-53136-7. —ISBN 0-471-53137-5 (pbk.)
    1. Engineers—Employment. 2. Technicians in industry—Employment.
    3. Job hunting.   I. Title.
    TA157.M595   1991
    602.3—dc20   91-8002

PREFACE

For nearly 14 years I have assisted companies in identifying and hiring technical personnel. While my primary area is the computer and information systems industries, I have also performed searches for engineers and technical sales and marketing representatives across the spectrum from entry to executive level.

Search activities involve much more than merely finding people with specific qualifications. Each person is an individual who must interact satisfactorily with possible employers. As I identify possible candidates for positions, I help them present themselves in the best manner possible to their prospective employers. Over the years, I have interviewed several thousand possible candidates and subsequently arranged interviews for many of them.

I have seen these candidates do many things right and many things wrong. I have seen them make mistakes in their interviews and lose excellent opportunities. On the other hand, I have seen them do everything right and still not get the jobs. In some cases, candidates got the jobs in spite of interviews in which nothing seemed to go right.

I have advised candidates as to how they should conduct themselves throughout the job search in order to maximize their results. My approach has been to share my observations about what works and what does not. The bottom line is that those who have listened and followed my advice have had a significantly higher success rate at obtaining job offers than those who have not.

This book is a collection of my observations regarding techniques and strategies that work for technical professionals in their job searches. These techniques *do* work. When they are applied, more and higher offers are obtained. I have included time-honored methods, personal opinion, and observations that will improve the job seeker's chances of success. Also included are true stories of successes and failures. I have changed the names of the people, companies, and places in the stories, but the facts are true.

At the end of the book is a "Selected Bibliography and Recommended Reading List." I have intentionally included many books of the career and job search genre because I believe that job seekers are best served by taking a broad approach to the abundance of advice that exists on the subject. According to the claims most of these books make on their jackets, no other information is necessary if you follow their advice. I do not buy this, but I *do* believe that each has a perspective worth considering, and the more information you have the better the conclusions you will reach regarding the most effective tactics to use. I had occasion to call one of the authors on the list (I won't say which), and he told me that his was the only book on the market worth reading. He told me he was going to open an office in Southern California, but not to tell his competitors because the knowledge would intimidate them. As arrogant as his attitude is, I feel he has written a book worth reading, so I have included it.

The focus of this book is on the technical professional. The goal is to expand and improve his or her nontechnical skills pertaining to the job search. These include communication and interpersonal skills that help job hunters to project and sell their technical abilities. These skills include interviewing, listening, and projecting a favorable image. Most books on the job search concentrate on areas such as résumé preparation and ever-popular questions to expect on an interview. These have been handled elsewhere, and while I have dealt with résumés and interview interaction here, I have done so based on my experience and observations, rather than passing along the standard verbiage. My opinion of résumés is not high, and my approach is to recognize their shortcomings while using them to the job seeker's advantage.

When I undertook the task of writing a book on the job search for technical people, I determined that I would not pull any punches and would tell it the way I saw it. I have made an effort to provide tough talk and straight advice from a technical search professional to technical professionals regarding their career paths. Too often, I have observed that technical people get buried in obsolete or limited technology or in the performance of assignments in which they will find themselves in a dead end. To avoid this, they need skills not taught in technical curricula, skills such as technology evaluation, career positioning, job market analysis, and knowing when and how to seek a different opportunity.

The person who will benefit most from this book is the technical professional preparing to find a job. The term *technical professional* includes the broad spectrum of people who work with technology. Included are engineers, scientists, technicians, medical personnel, computer specialists, and technical support people. The book will be of value to both entry-level and senior-level professionals. It will be an especially valuable handbook for new graduates embarking on a technical career.

While technical professionals are the target audience, the techniques and observations are just as valid for anyone else conducting a job search. It will also be valuable for employers who are hiring technical personnel.

Because my personal experience is in the third-party search and placement area, I have included a chapter on how to use the services of those in my industry to your best advantage.

My advice to the job seeker is to read this book to learn from and use its lessons. Also read other materials and integrate their lessons into your personal skill mix. Use the ideas that work best for you and reject those that don't. Your goal is to find the best career opportunity. Give it your best shot, and good luck!

DAVID J. MOORE

San Juan Capistrano, California
July 1991

ACKNOWLEDGMENTS

My thanks go out to the candidates and companies with whom I have dealt over the years. My experiences with them have formed my attitudes and served as the catalysts to developing the techniques presented here in this book. I am most grateful to my loving wife Amelia, who tolerated my frustrations and encouraged my successes. She also was a receptive and patient listener to the many ideas I tossed around as I considered what was to be included in the book.

Colleagues and associates in the search industry have shared their skills with me and mentored me, and I am grateful for their help and contributions.

D.J.M.

TRADEMARKS

Arriba is a trademark of Good Software Corporation.

Canon and LBP are registered trademarks of Canon Inc.

dBASE, dBASE III, and dBASE IV are registered trademarks of Ashton-Tate Corporation.

Hewlett-Packard, HP, and LaserJet are registered trademarks of Hewlett-Packard Co.

IBM is a registered trademark of International Business Machines

Lotus, 1-2-3, and Agenda are registered trademarks of Lotus Development Corporation.

OnTime is a registered trademark of Campbell Services Inc.

Paradox, Sidekick, and Quattro Pro are registered trademarks of Borland International, Inc.

The Perfect Résumé Computer Kit is a registered trademark of Permax Systems Inc.

Prodigy is a registered trademark of Prodigy Services Co.

Q&A is a trademark of Symantek Corporation.

R:BASE is a registered trademark of Microrim, Inc.

RésuméMaker is a trademark of Individual Software, Inc.

The Selling System and It's About Time are trademarks of Pyramid Software Inc.

Toastmasters is a registered trademark of Toastmasters International Inc.

Totall Manager is a registered trademark of Bartell Software.

WordPerfect is a registered trademark of WorkPerfect Corporation.

WordStar is a registered trademark and Advanced Page Preview is a trademark of WordStar International Incorporated.

CONTENTS

1

SELF-ESTEEM SEARCH

The Success Factor in the Job

T here is no secret ingredient in a successful job search. If there were one word to describe it, it would be *attitude.* Whether you call it "self-esteem," "confidence," or "determination," it is the ingredient that will ensure success in any endeavor.

WHY FEELING GOOD ABOUT YOURSELF IS IMPORTANT TO THE JOB SEARCH

Job hunting and job changing are among the highest stress-producing activities in life. If you are currently out of work, you are experiencing the anxiety of not knowing whether you are going to work or where, economic pressures, family turmoil, and a loss of self-esteem. If you have been out of work in the past, you understand the stress and know it is not pleasant.

If you are seeking and evaluating new opportunities in the process of changing jobs, you are also experiencing stress. Whether it is negative or positive stress depends on the conditions under which you are conducting your search. If you are happy in your current job and are only evaluating potential opportunities, the stress is minimal; the greatest stress will occur when one of those opportunities becomes a reality and you are faced with a choice between your current job and the new employment. If your current job is unpleasant and you feel driven to find another job, the stress can be intense.

A close friend recently changed jobs because of what he perceived to be an oppressive employer. The employer made promises about compensation, support, and work conditions, then broke them, dangling the carrot, then pulling it back. My friend was pushed to work extra hours, was called in on weekends, had social plans disrupted, and was belittled and intimidated verbally. The pressure he felt to find a different job was extremely high. His field was sales and technical support of computer software, and at the time he was looking there were not many jobs available. I could offer few assignments in his field; my clients were looking for different skills and a different level of expertise than my friend possessed.

The stress was terrible. My friend called me daily to unload his feelings and tell me of the frustrations he was experiencing in his job search. The stress came from two directions: The pressure from his present job continued while the stress from the job search added to the tension. He missed several days of work because of various illnesses ranging from fatigue to stomach flu. The worry and strain showed in his face, and I counseled him not to carry that look into his interviews. In order to succeed in an interview, it is vital that the candidate not exhibit anxiety in front of a potential employer. Employers offer jobs because they believe the candidate can do the job, and the candidate must instill that confidence.

It was not a pleasant experience for my friend, but I'm pleased to say he has a new position and is very happy. His comment was, "It was like hitting my head against a wall, but it felt so good after it was over that I was glad I did it."

THE KEY: SELF-ESTEEM

High self-esteem is the key to success in all things, including job and career success. It is another way of saying you feel good about yourself. You are pleased with your performance and your life. You feel that things are going well for you, and you translate that feeling into a confidence that you can whip the world. However, problems such as loss of a job, being passed over for a promotion, suffering financial reversals, being chewed out by a boss, family problems, and unfulfilled career goals can assault your self-esteem and cause you to question your self-worth.

Technical professionals generally have high self-esteem. They have much going for them. They are generally intelligent and well educated, hold prestigious positions, and earn high salaries. They have good reasons to feel good about themselves. When they have problems and their personal or professional well-being is threatened, however, they become vulnerable and their self-esteem suffers.

Realizing that self-esteem is essential to success is the first step to gaining control of it. This knowledge enables us to be alert to circumstances that could be damaging to the perception of our self-worth and reinforce those factors that enhance it.

A WORD OF CAUTION

Technical professionals place great stock in their technical skills and abilities. If they engage in self-improvement activities, it is likely to be in the form of attending technical seminars or programs supporting their professional field. Technical people are usually not found at motivational seminars and meetings, which are more likely to attract participants from people-oriented professions such as sales or management. This doesn't mean that technical professionals don't need to be motivated; rather, they tend to concentrate their training in the realm of their technical specialties.

Professionals in people-oriented occupations understand the need to be in high spirits. They know that they must be "up" in order to succeed, and they are open to knowledge and techniques that will enable them to achieve that state. Technical professionals need the same high spirits, and as long as their career and personal lives are going well, they have them. The motivational techniques that work for non-technical people also work for the technical people.

My word of caution for the technical professional is this: Don't think that you can get along without a motivational and spiritual boost from time to time. Realize that the time you will need the most self-esteem will be the time that you feel the worst—when you are out of work or in a job in which things are not going well. Knowing what to do to raise your self-esteem is a valuable asset.

HOW TO BUILD AND MAINTAIN YOUR SELF-ESTEEM

There are a number of positive steps you can take to ensure that your self-esteem remains at its peak.

1. *Face your problems with as little emotion as possible.* When misfortune strikes, crying about it will not resolve the problem. Complaining, being angry with yourself or others, or allowing yourself to sink into a state of depression will do nothing to correct the situation. Put the problem behind you as quickly as possible and get on with your life.

Let me interject a thought here. I realize that getting kicked in the face emotionally is not easy to put behind you. When I get angry and hurt, I rant and rave and blow off steam. But I also know that it doesn't help a bit except emotionally. Psychologists will tell you that suppressing your emotions is unhealthy and will lead to more problems later on. Therefore, while you must put your problems behind you as quickly as possible, you must also find an outlet for your feelings.

2. *Vent your feelings, but do it in a healthy way.* The best way I have found to vent feelings is to exercise. Go running, jogging, walking, or whatever you prefer to work up a sweat and wear yourself out. I go on long walks and talk to myself. With no one around, I make speeches, tell off the people who have angered me, and even yell into the wind. Afterwards I feel better, and with my emotions cooled off I have a clearer head to think about my problems.

3. *Forgive!* Forgive the people you might blame for your problems, but most of all, forgive yourself. Most of our problems can be traced back to something that is of our own doing, and neither self-deprecation nor getting mad at the world will make things any better.

Forgiveness is a wonderful cure for emotional problems. However, there is one firm rule that must be applied. It must be unconditional. You cannot demand that either others or yourself meet some requirement or perform an act of contrition before you grant forgiveness. Forgiveness is for your benefit, not for the other person. If you cannot forgive yourself, you will only drive yourself deeper into a miserable state.

4. *Lay out a plan to raise your self-esteem* and *achieve your career goals.* This is a big order, one that could be overwhelming even if you weren't down emotionally. I was once told that if you want to eat an elephant, take small bites. Breaking your plan down into more manageable pieces will enable you to accomplish it more easily. Life can be viewed as comprising several areas, and that is how I recommend that you structure your plan. These areas are family, social life, work, financial affairs, and physical and spiritual well-being.

If you are looking for a job, it is important to put your life in as good order as possible so you can put maximum effort into your job search. If your life is in order, then you feel good about it and your self-esteem is high. Your family will also be more secure and supportive.

5. *Lay out a budget that will support your job search.* Assume that it will take approximately one week for every year of experience or one month for every $10,000 of income, whichever is higher. Three to six months for a comprehensive job search is not unusual, so don't cut yourself short. If you are out of work during your job search, plan a lean budget and take a worst-case position.

Take inventory of your assets, including savings, any job hunt "war chest" you might have established, severance benefits, and other income that you might draw on during your job search. Consider all the resources you might have to use in order to reach your goals.

6. *Sit down with your family and include them in your planning process.* They are dependent on your success, they love you, and they should be a part of whatever choices you make.

7. *Find a mentor or friend to whom you can confide feelings about your job search and career plans.* This person should be close enough that you can vent your emotions and get any negative feelings out of your system. Also, the person should be someone for whom you have sufficient respect that you would be willing to consider any advice offered.

8. *Work on developing your network.* Call your friends and current business associates and tell them your plans and goals. Meet them for lunch, attend association meetings, and reach out to people who might view you as a customer (perhaps they have made money through your efforts).

9. *Develop your job hunting and interpersonal skills.* Read books and attend seminars on interviewing and job search techniques. Watch motivational videos and listen to tapes. Open yourself to skills outside your technical background. Seek a more liberal education. I have been told that if you read five good books on any subject, you can be considered an expert because you will be more knowledgeable about that subject than 99 percent of the population.

10. *Establish a daily schedule and follow it.* If you are employed, you already follow a schedule set down by your employer. Devote at least two hours each evening to your job search. This should include research on companies, letter writing, and networking.

If you are not working, following a daily schedule is an absolute must. You must arise at a set time, and "go to work." A job search is the hardest and most important job you will ever have, and you are working for your toughest boss—yourself. Discipline is necessary or your job search will falter and your self-esteem will erode. I recommend that you also *dress* as if you were going to work. Establish a work schedule and keep records.

11. *Believe in yourself!* You know yourself and your strengths. The bottom line of self-esteem is how we view ourselves, but oddly enough, our self-esteem is affected by the way we think others view us. When we are out of work, we tend to think that others see us as less worthy than if we had a job. A job gives us status. This is compounded by the uncertainty that comes from not knowing when a suitable position will be found.

It is crucial to remember that you are the same person unemployed as you were when you had a job. You have the same skills and talents; the only difference is how you view yourself, and that view is self-esteem. Unless you have done something disgraceful that caused you to lose your job, you have no reason to feel less worthy than you did when you were working.

12. *Understand that everyone who looks for work will find work.* Moreover, 95 percent of those who find work will find more satisfying work at higher pay.

How you feel about yourself is your responsibility and yours alone. No one else can be blamed. If you have ever driven a car and been cut off by an inconsiderate driver, you know that you can yell at the other driver, get angry, and have your blood pressure go through the ceiling, but it will only have an adverse effect on you. The other driver will drive on and very likely never know how angry you were. How you react in any situation is your choice, and the same is true of self-esteem. You make a conscious choice to feel good. What others think of you has no effect—physical or mental—on you. Actually, most people's perception of you hasn't changed at all, regardless of your circumstances. The change is in what *you think* they think about you.

FORMULA FOR A POSITIVE ATTITUDE

One of the best thoughts I ever heard on building a positive attitude was structured around an acrostic. An acrostic or acronym is a word formed from the first letters of a series of words or sentences. Many organizations use this technique. For example, the anti-drinking-and-driving organization MADD stands for *Mothers Against Drunk Driving*. This acrostic formed the outline for the sermon of a visiting preacher at a church service I attended about 20 years ago. Here is the formula for a positive attitude and high self-esteem. The word is

WATCH

Let's break it down into its acrostic.

W means watch your **WORDS.**

Words are important. Nations have gone to war over words, and words have brought peace. The wisdom and great literature of the world are preserved in words.

Words are essential for self-esteem. What people say to you and what you say to them will determine the quality of your relationship with them and their attitudes toward you. Words also define how you feel about yourself.

Résumés, feature-accomplishment-benefit presentations (F-A-Bs), cover letters, follow-up letters, and acceptance letters are made up of words, and words comprise what you say in a job interview.

A means watch your **ACTIONS.**

"Actions speak louder than words," or so goes the old cliché. It also happens to be true. There's another old cliché, "If it looks like a duck, walks like a duck, and quacks like a duck, chances are it *is* a duck!" You can say many things and make many promises and claims, but if your actions do not match them, your words are empty and meaningless.

How you conduct yourself in interviews (or in any area of your life) will tell people who you are and how you feel about yourself far more clearly than what you say. If you hold yourself erect and walk as if you owned the world, people will believe that you do, because that is what your actions tell them.

T means watch your **THOUGHTS.**

Too often, words and actions come across as if there were no thought at all behind them. This is why it is important to think before you speak or act.

Many years ago, Norman Vincent Peale wrote a book titled *The Power of Positive Thinking* (Prentice-Hall, 1954). Its premise was that a positive outlook and "can do" spirit would provide the impetus to overcome obstacles and accomplish difficult tasks. Dr. Peale promoted the idea of belief in yourself. Today there are techniques available to help you believe in yourself. One of these is visualization, a technique whereby you go beyond daydreaming to place yourself into real-life situations and "see" yourself succeeding.

The question of whether you can actually "think" your way to success may be open to discussion. However, my position is that I would rather go into any predicament believing I can succeed than having self-doubts and worrying about failing. There's sufficient evidence to believe that thinking positively about your life *can* make a difference.

C means watch your **COMPANIONS.**

The people you associate with determine in large measure how others view you. If you make it your business to associate with successful people, you will be identified with them and considered to be a winner also. If you are continually seen with losers, you will be viewed as being part of that group. How people view you determines how they treat you and respond to you.

Picking winners is not that difficult. At work they are the rising stars. I don't mean the manipulators or the smooth talkers; I am talking about the hard workers and the people who are looked to as mentors. Seek their guidance and respect.

Join associations of professionals in your technical specialty. Be a participant. Serve on committees, hold offices, and join in association activities. Soon you will be one of the people others seek out and consider to be a winner.

H means watch your **HEART.**

In our society, "heart" is the expression we use for "inner being," "soul," and "personality." Phrases such as "Your heart's in the right place," "You gotta have heart," and "My heart aches for you" convey some of the meanings attached to this word. In the context of self-esteem, heart is the essence of what you are or what you believe you are. It is who you are when all the pretense is stripped away. It is how you view yourself and what you believe—your value system and the person you present to the rest of the world.

Words, actions, thoughts, and companions can mislead you, but your heart never can. You might be able to fool others, but you cannot fool yourself. If your heart is not right, you are not right. Heart is the key to self-esteem.

That's the formula. Remember it and use it.

Watch your *Words.*
Watch your *Actions.*
Watch your *Thoughts.*
Watch your *Companions.*
Watch your *Heart.*
WATCH!

SUMMARY

Self-esteem is the bottom line in job search success. In fact, it is the key to success in any endeavor. The steps to building and maintaining self-esteem are as follows:

1. Face problems squarely with a minimum of emotion.

2. Don't bottle up your emotions. Release your feelings, but in a positive and healthy way such as exercise.

3. Forgive the people who may be to blame for your troubles. The most important person to forgive is yourself. Forgive unconditionally.

4. Start making plans to reach your career goals. The simple act of establishing goals will make it easier for you to see where you are going and will give your self-esteem and self-worth a boost.

5. Be realistic. There's going to be a cost in time and money, and you will do better if you prepare a budget and examine the costs you must incur in order to succeed.

6. Include family and friends in your planning process.

7. Develop your network.

8. Develop your job search and interpersonal communications skills.

9. Cultivate a daily schedule and routine.

10. Believe in yourself.

11. Keep in mind that everyone who looks for work will find work.

Finally, remember to WATCH!

2

PROFILE OF
THE TECHNICAL
PROFESSIONAL

What is a technical professional? Are technical professionals different from other people in the job market? Do they view themselves as different? What are the differences? What are the similarities?

WHAT IS A TECHNICAL PROFESSIONAL?

A professional is a person who performs or works for pay. *Technical* defines skills in a particular field. While technical ability is commonly identified with disciplines such as engineering that are associated with mechanical sciences, it can be broadened to include skills of almost any endeavor.

Engineers and computer specialists are unquestionably technical professionals. However, this definition can be extended to anyone who seeks perfection in a chosen field. A musician who is especially adept on an instrument might be described as a "technician." Working in trades such as carpentry or plumbing requires technical skills, and an accomplished practitioner would certainly deserve being called a technician. Therefore, a technician in the broadest sense is a person who is good at whatever his or her work might be.

Another definition might be the concentration of skill-building in a single area without regard for its interaction with other areas of interest. Computer specialists who seek to perfect their knowledge and make a computer perform to its maximum would certainly qualify as technicians, although some might call them "hackers." I knew a computer programmer whose greatest love was making a computer perform. He would program for the sheer joy of watching the program run. His primary aim was to increase his own proficiency. His goal was to become as technically proficient as possible without regard for nontechnical concerns.

THE TECHNICAL ENVIRONMENT

The one thing that distinguishes the technical working environment from other working environments is its focus on things rather than people. I realize there are other people involved in even the purest science. However, the technician's interest is not in the people but in the skills needed to work in the field.

Technical professionals operate best in an environment of "things" for three reasons. First, they have been educated in the knowledge and skills of a technical field. Second, they are expert in a technical field because that is where they work. Third, they work in a technical field because that is what they enjoy and prefer to do.

"People" skills are not necessarily considered requirements for technical proficiency. They are useful in any job, but they are usually considered to be more important for salespeople or managers than for technicians. Don't get me wrong. Many technical professionals are proficient in "people" skills. Many who progress into management positions either already have these skills or learn them in order to succeed.

One appropriate definition for the technical environment is the view of those who work in it. If people who work there consider it as technical, then it is. This gives a broader definition than the workplace and conditions of engineering, computers, or other science-based professions. I like it best because it is not forced from the outside but reflects how those who work in a field prefer to view themselves.

MYTHS AFFECTING
THE TECHNICAL PROFESSIONAL

Whether they are accurate or not, the self-image of technical people, and the way in which they are viewed by others affect the perception technical people have about themselves and how they react to their working environment. While stereotypes have some basis in fact, an examination of how technical professionals are viewed will provide insight to how they feel about themselves.

How Nontechnical People View Technical Professionals

Nontechnical people conjure up a variety of images of their technical counterparts. From the time they are in grammar school, bright students who lean toward scientific interests are called "brains," "eggheads," "nerds," and a number of other uncomplimentary terms. In the workplace, they are called "propeller heads."

As with most other prejudices, there is little factual evidence to support these views; they amount to outright bigotry. Technical people rightfully resent such attitudes. Because they work in jobs that focus on the discipline rather than people, they are often viewed as being introverts. This may or may not be the case, but all technical professionals will suffer from being tarred with this brush.

How Technical Professionals View Themselves

Technical people view themselves in a variety of ways. Some accept the "propeller head" image either with a perverse sense of pride or with righteous indignation. Others consider their technical talents and positions with justified pride.

The Truth About Technical Professionals

Are technical professionals really different? The answer is both yes and no. Yes—Their technical skills and talents set them apart. And no—People are individuals with separate personalities, and they seldom fall into the molds others make for them. Technical professionals are no different from other people. They are introverts and extroverts, good and bad, rich and poor. They are individuals with the same values as others in the society.

THE TECHNICAL PROFESSIONAL AND THE JOB SEARCH

The employment market has a special place for the technical professional. Technical jobs are among the most complex and difficult. When the technical professional steps into this arena, the job requirements are more stringent and the qualifications more demanding than for other professions. Employers tend to insist on the top candidates, and the competition for the best jobs is keen.

This does not imply that employers of nontechnical people are not just as demanding in their quest for the best candidates. It simply means that technical jobs are universally tough and candidates are evaluated more critically with the precise yardstick of technology.

Truth and Misconception

One thing that is true about the job search in every case— technical and nontechnical alike—is that *every person who looks for work will find work.* This is axiomatic. There is no way to predict how much time it will take before a job is found or what salary will be offered, but it is a sure bet that the candidate who perseveres will find a job.

Use and Misuse of Job Search Tools

If asked to list the tools of the job search, the average person would very likely exhibit a blank stare. However, there are many tools available to assist the job seeker. The list includes résumés, networks, advertising, libraries, telephones, laws, and so on. Whether job hunters recognize it or not, how they use or misuse these tools will impact the success or failure of their job search.

Actually, attitude is the key. A job seeker who exaggerates qualifications or puts an outright lie on a résumé may believe it is the right thing to do, but the results can be devastating. Failing to take advantage of library research resources or wasting time answering ads that yield nothing can lead to no job prospects.

If there is a secret or key to finding a job, it is the attitude the job hunter has about the job search. A positive attitude will succeed in every case. I have seen people who were literally down to their last dollar approach their job search with the confidence of a millionaire. I also know people at the other end of the spectrum.

Consider Bill. Bill owned four houses, had a credit line over $400,000, and had no debts. After being out of work for three months, he called and told me that if he didn't find a job within another month, he'd be on the street. Interview after interview turned sour. I arranged three interviews for him, and the feedback I received from the employers with whom he interviewed was revealing. He openly expressed doubts about his abilities. His posture and body language were those of a frightened and beaten man. He could barely look the interviewers in the eye. He stumbled over his words and became agitated and emotional after each interview.

Bill finally got a job after five months. It was not the job he wanted, but, as he put it, "It paid the bills." He is still depressed and frightened. He still has his houses and no debts, but he would trade it all for a couple of ounces of confidence and self-esteem. I think it would be worth it.

THE MESSAGE FOR TECHNICAL PROFESSIONALS

There is a special message in this book for technical professionals. It is not that they should approach the business of finding a job differently from the rest of the population. Rather, it is that the same techniques that work for all other successful job seekers work for technical professionals. Using them will help technical professionals maximize their efforts and find the best jobs available.

SUMMARY

A technical professional is a person who works for compensation in a field or discipline in which the primary emphasis is on things rather than people. While the concept of being technical is generally associated with scientific disciplines, it may encompass a broader spectrum and is best defined by those persons who perceive themselves as "technical."

As with most stereotypes, the view that technical professionals are introverted nonconformists who are not "people" people and lack the social graces of their nontechnical counterparts is not supported by facts and can be properly labeled as bigotry. Most technical professionals are proud of their technical skills and resent any erroneous views that might be held of them. The truth is that technical professionals do not fall into categories or stereotypes any more than other groups of people with similar skills and interests. They are individuals with a wide range of values.

Because of the high demands of technical disciplines and the rigorous requirements of technical jobs, technical professionals face some different circumstances in the job search. In addition to being assessed as persons, they will be measured even more stringently according to the technological standards of their chosen discipline.

An important message for the technical professional is that attitude is the key factor in the successful job search. While technical expertise is still a primary ingredient, a strong positive attitude is essential for success. The successful job hunting technical professional will have to master the tools and techniques of the job search as well as having topnotch skills in his or her technical discipline.

3

THE TECHNICAL JOB SEARCH

Planning, Preparation, and Execution

I know a job hunter who claims that he's never had to look for a job. According to him, he has always been sought out by employers and has had a choice of desirable positions. That is, until he called me.

My business is searching and recruiting. I receive search assignments from employer clients and then search out and recruit qualified candidates for the positions. This particular candidate had nearly 20 years of work experience and had experienced neither the joy nor the pain of a job search. When his current company was bought out and relocated and he chose not to go, there was no one seeking to hire him. For 20 years he had allowed the desires of other people to drive his career. While I'm certain he did not plan it that way, the ease with which work had found him in the past proved to be a disservice as he began his job search. His motive in calling me was to shift the burden of planning and executing his job search to a third-party recruiter. The important point for this candidate (or any other job seeker) to learn is that the task of finding a job cannot be passed along to someone else. You have to do it yourself.

This chapter is an overview of the job search in the technical marketplace. It is an anatomical view of the job search process. Technical professionals are familiar with the concept of analysis, which involves addressing an overall process by breaking it down into more easily identifiable and manageable pieces. Analysis is the scientific way of saying, "If you want to eat an elephant, take small bites."

In addition to viewing the job search as made up of individual components, there are three other dimensions that must be superimposed on the process. These are planning, preparation, and execution. As in any endeavor requiring skill and intelligence, merely knowing the components of the job search and how they work is not enough, just as knowing how an airplane is built and the principles of aerodynamics is not enough to successfully fly it. In order to put the individual parts together to form a successful job search, it is also necessary to know how to *plan* the job search, how to *prepare* for it, and how to *execute* it or carry it out.

The following is an old Arab proverb that has been loosely translated into English:

> The best of all possible situations is to know that you know.
> The next best situation is to know that you don't know.
> It is less desirable to not know that you know.
> But the worst of all possible situations is not to know that you don't know.[1]

Success in a job search is achieved through an understanding of the components that make up the search followed by careful and correct execution. This seems simple enough, but like most simple formulas it's easier said than done. Let's take a look at what makes a job search.

---

[1]Anonymous. From Thomas J. Martin, Jr., *Malice in Blunderland* (New York: McGraw-Hill, 1973), p. 39.

PLANNING

Planning is the key to success in any undertaking, and there are few undertakings as important as a job search. Finding and landing a job that will take up the majority of your waking hours, provide the income that determines your standard of living, and provide the experience from which you will proceed to the remainder of your career is more than hard work—it is one of the most important things you will ever do.

The job search component that causes you to start looking for a job or a change in jobs is *need.* Until you have no job or become unhappy in your current job, it is unlikely that you will become sufficiently motivated to begin planning. Need manifests itself in a number of ways. The most traumatic is the sudden loss of your job. When it comes without warning, it can be devastating. Fortunately, this seldom occurs. There are normally warning signs such as loss of business, poor financial reports, merger and buyout talk, and changes in attitude toward you. When any of these become real enough, the idea that you should start looking elsewhere usually enters your mind.

In the case of sudden job loss, there is shock followed by the numbing realization that you are no longer employed. The thought of what you will do next does not occur immediately. As with most other traumatic experiences, you will go through the five stages described by Elisabeth Kubler-Ross in her book *On Death and Dying.*[2] The five stages are (1) denial—"No, not me!"; (2) rage and anger—"Why me?"; (3) bargaining—"Yes, me but . . ."; (4) depression—"Yes, me"; and (5) acceptance—"I understand and it's all right."

These stages are not fixed in concrete. Depending on the level of trauma experienced, you may move to acceptance with barely a hint of the other stages or you may be consumed by one or more of the stages such as rage and anger or depression. Recognizing that these feelings are likely to occur is helpful in meeting and dealing with them. Ideally, you

---

[2] Elisabeth Kubler-Ross, *On Death and Dying* (New York: Harper and Row, 1973).

must move as quickly as possible to acceptance so you can do something positive about getting back to work. Your attitude and level of preparedness will determine how quickly you reach this point of moving forward with your life.

At a professional association meeting one evening, I sat next to Tom, the manager of a development group for a computer manufacturer. He was somewhat depressed, but not because he had lost his job. That day he had laid off or terminated 33 people out of 35 in his group. His depression was not because of the layoff—he had known about it for six months and had accepted it. A decision had been made to relocate the corporate headquarters out of state and leave only a small support staff at the current site. These plans were passed to the staff, as well as new information when it became available.

What amazed and depressed Tom was the variety of responses from his staff. All had initially expressed shock and denial. Some took the news in stride and started making plans. The company offered relocation as one option, and several chose it. Others started actively looking for another job. About 25 percent believed that the company would change its mind or that they would not be let go. Tom said that as D-Day grew closer and it became evident that the move was a reality, most employees rapidly moved through anger to acceptance. The one sight Tom said he would never forget was a senior engineer who had been with the company for over ten years. The man believed up to the last day that he would somehow be spared. The last time Tom saw him was in the company parking lot. He was standing by his car with a cardboard box full of personal items from his desk. He and his wife and two small children were crying. He had finally realized it was true.

This is unfortunate. If ever the truth, however unpleasant, must be faced, it is in job situations. How many opportunities had this man missed? How long would he continue to grieve until he got his life back together? Tom felt a sense of responsibility, not just because he was the manager, but because he had tried vigorously to convince the man.

Whatever your motivation is, recognize it, get through the emotions, and start planning.

Set Goals

Recognition of a need is the first step in establishing a goal. If you wanted to travel to a strange city and were asked how you would get there, the first question you would ask is "Where am I now?" You cannot possibly establish a route until you know your starting point. As logical as this sounds, people all too often launch into a job search without determining where they are at the beginning.

A need tells you that you want to go somewhere. A goal expresses where you want to go. Determination of where you are combined with where you want to go is the key to planning. By looking at the terrain between the two points, your planning will consist of determining what route you will take and what equipment you will need for the journey.

Take Inventory

No technician would begin a job without the right tools. Finding employment is the most important job you will ever undertake. Tools are so vital to some jobs that they cannot be done without them. Can you imagine a surgeon attempting an operation without a scalpel or a carpenter building a house without a hammer and saw? Stepping out on a job search without being properly equipped is like going hunting without a gun—unthinkable!

The first step is to take inventory of yourself. What do you have to offer a prospective employer? Most people have a résumé of some sort. However, résumés are at best only support tools. No one ever got hired from one. For now, please take my word that you must go farther than the résumé in your self-inventory.

The best tool for self-assessment is the F-A-B presentation. *F-A-B* stands for "feature-accomplishment-benefit." This tool will enable you to probe into your abilities and accomplishments, then present them in the most effective manner. A discussion of the mechanics and use of the F-A-B presentation is found in Chapter 4. An F-A-B is not a résumé. Both are marketing tools, but the résumé is seriously flawed and may work to your disadvantage. This will also be discussed in Chapter 4.

Look to the future. What would you *really* like to do? Go ahead and let your imagination run wild! You now have the opportunity to determine what you will do for the rest of your life. Before you decided to change jobs (or the choice was forced on you), your life was going in a different direction. Even if it was in the direction you wanted, you didn't have this opportunity before you.

Some of your choices may not be financially or even technically possible. What an exercise like this will do is force you to take a look at where you want to go. Following on the heels of constructing your F-A-B, this an excellent way to define or review your goals. In some cases, you may choose a new path.

Use Your Network

Most people get their jobs through someone they know. The process is called *networking,* and it is the most powerful and effective tool in the job hunter's repertoire.

It's likely that you know quite a few people and already have an established network. As a technical professional, you've worked in your field and know co-workers and managers. You've also met people who were in school with you training for the same field. There are also your instructors and professors. You may not have used the network in a job search before, but that is just a matter of knowing how. You can also expand your network to great advantage in other areas of your professional life.

Expand Your Muscles and Your Mind

With the exception of two, every invention in human history has been of the muscle-expanding variety. The wheel, fulcrum, and screw were among the earliest; they were designed to give human beings a longer reach and increased strength. Even weapons were designed with the single idea of extending reach. Modern devices have only improved our ability to go faster, see or hear better, or lift more. The airplane makes each of us a Superman able "to leap tall buildings at a single bound." Cars enable us to race effortlessly at many times the speed we could walk or run. Television, radio, and the telephone give us the ability to see, hear, or talk without geographical limitations.

There have only been two inventions that could be called "mind stretching." These are the printing press and the computer. The personal computer (PC) or one of its cousins can stretch your reach into the job search marketplace, giving you abilities that were formerly available only to large organizations. This is due to the relatively low cost of PC systems and the wide variety of software available. Chapter 5 examines in detail some of the hardware and software that you can use to your advantage.

Hone Your Job Search Skills

Searching for a job is much more difficult than performing the job itself. If you tried to perform at a technical job without the necessary skills, you would not be surprised if you failed. You're not just trying to find a job. You're going after the best possible job that fits your skills and background and the one that will best meet your career goals. You want to ensure that you will succeed. You can't afford not to, because your way of life and your measurements of success or failure are riding on it. You want the best equipment available.

Job hunting skills consist of interviewing skills, interpersonal and written communication skills, knowledge of the marketplace, ability to present yourself favorably, and ability to generate and exploit contacts.

It is a fact of life that people are not hired (or fired) because of their technical ability. This does not mean that technical qualifications are not necessary; on the contrary, they are vital to job success. It means that employers hire people based on their ability to present themselves and communicate the competence the employers are seeking. Furthermore, employers hire people they like. If this sounds discriminatory, it is. Regardless of the law, social pressure, or court-ordered mandates, employers are going to hire candidates they like, although they will do it within the law. It boils down to the fact that if you cannot communicate your ability to do the job and do it in a pleasing way to a prospective employer, you will not be hired.

In planning for a job search, take inventory of your interpersonal and communication skills. Benchmark where you are, and set out to improve. Remember, regardless of where you are, there is always room for improvement.

PREPARATION

Now that you know where you are, your job goal is clear, and you have a plan for getting there, you must prepare for the task at hand. This will include a determination of companies you will target for possible positions; preparation of your communication package to include your résumé, your F-A-B, cover letters, thank-you letters, and follow-up letters; honing of your interview and verbal communication skills, and setup of computer assistance. Oh yes, you might also review your technical strengths and weaknesses to see where they fit into your goals.

Résumés and F-A-Bs

The résumé is a marketing tool used by job hunters to introduce themselves to prospective employers. In Chapter 4 I will discuss the use and preparation of the résumé in depth, but for now suffice it to say that it is an imperfect device and is given far more attention than it deserves. Because it is viewed as a necessity by the majority of buyers in the employment marketplace, you must have one. The knowledge that résumés are generally misused can work in your favor. An understanding of the dynamics of résumé usage will enable you to prepare yours so that it works to your best advantage.

The feature-accomplishment-benefit, or F-A-B, presentation is a much better tool for marketing and personal introduction than the résumé—especially for the technical professional. The mechanics of preparing an F-A-B are covered in detail in Chapter 4. As a marketing device, it is a powerful tool for telling employers how you can benefit their organizations.

Required Correspondence

There are three letters you will send to every employer with whom you have an interview. These are the *cover letter*, the *thank-you letter*, and the *follow-up letter*.

The Cover Letter

The cover letter is included in all written correspondence that is used to introduce you to a prospective employer. Its importance is heightened by the fact that it is probably the first look an employer will get at you or your work. This demands that it carry a powerful message, one that will grab the reader and demand attention and action. The construction of effective cover letters, including examples, is covered in Chapter 4.

The Thank-You Letter

Less than 5 percent of all job seekers send a thank-you letter to the person with whom they interviewed. Aside from its being a common courtesy, the fact that so few do it means that those who *do* give themselves an edge over those who don't.

In some cases you might be the top candidate and would be hired regardless of whether you sent a thank-you letter. If you are interested in the position and plan to accept the job, a thank-you letter is a positive way to get off on the right foot with your new boss.

At the other end of the spectrum, the interview may not have gone well at all. In this case, a thank-you letter affirms that you are a courteous person. Technical communities tend to be small, and if the last thing an employer remembers about you is receiving a pleasant thank-you letter, it will not hurt your reputation. I have also seen the thank-you letter cause the employer to reevaluate a job candidate, resulting in a hire. In any case, writing a thank-you letter will never hurt you, and it has an excellent prospect of enhancing your chances to be hired.

If an employer is interviewing a large number of people, it is likely that no decision will be made until enough candidates have been interviewed so some kind of comparison can be made. If the employer gets a thank-you letter in the middle of the interview process, the person who sent it will stand out. Statistically, you will probably be the only candidate interviewed who sends a thank-you letter, and your chances of being remembered in a positive way increase.

The Follow-Up Letter

Follow-up letters can be used in several ways. You can send a letter a couple of weeks after the interview to update the employer on your status and restate your interest. This is a form of dunning letter, and it must be carefully stated to avoid that appearance. Follow-up letters can also be acceptance or pre-acceptance letters that lay out inquiries or concerns about the position. They may also be used six months or a year later to state continuing interest and inquire about employment opportunities. Samples of follow-up letters and how to prepare them are included in Chapter 4.

Interviews Preparation

Interviews is plural because a job interview is actually a series of interviews and you must prepare for each of them. There are telephone interviews, personnel interviews, screening interviews, technical interviews, executive interviews, exit interviews, and follow-up interviews.

Preparation is both physical and mental. *Physical* because in the face-to-face interview a good personal appearance is required in order to make a good first impression. *Mental* because interviews of all types are stressful and require not only that you be sharp and knowledgeable in your technical discipline, but also that you are knowledgeable about the prospective employer.

Preparing for an interview includes such areas as personal appearance, communication skills, and attitude, as well as telephone usage and having knowledge of the EEO (Equal Employment Opportunity) laws and regulations that might apply to you.

Physical Appearance

There's an old and hackneyed saying that "you never have a second chance to make a good first impression." As corny as that may sound, it is the absolute truth. People who believe that their technical abilities will get them a job and that physical appearance doesn't count are mistaken. It's true that employers expect strong technical backgrounds and that most job descriptions only emphasize the technical requirements. However, a favorable first impression that is the result of a good appearance adds to your chances of landing the job. Why take the chance of turning off an employer when a little attention to grooming and dress principles can give the employer good feelings about you from the start.

Chapter 9 discusses the interpersonal or "people" skills necessary to succeed in the job search. Dressing and image are among the most important of these skills.

Communication Skills

Communication skills are the most important and useful skills you can acquire. Even more important than technical abilities and knowledge is the ability to communicate well. If technical skills are equal, the candidate who can best communicate his or her technical ability will get the job.

The subject of communication will be discussed in detail in Chapter 6 and the specifics of interviewing in Chapter 8.

Attitude

If there were a single foundation on which to base success in both finding and performing a job, it would have to be mental attitude. Whether you call it self-esteem, "being up," or any other term, it is what enables the less qualified to snatch jobs away from the more technically adept.

I have known several job hunters who were literally down to their last dollar, yet their outward appearance and attitude were those of someone who was on top of the world. These people were always positive, and as a result they got jobs that were more satisfying and higher paying than the ones they held previously.

I have also known job hunters who were depressed at the idea of being out of a job. Not that joblessness isn't depressing, but crying about it will not help the situation. On the contrary, a sour, downcast attitude is the worst thing you can have for a job search.

EXECUTION

The best plans and preparation are of no value if the job search is poorly executed. A well-executed job search translates into a well-written F-A-B or résumé, a solid reach into an established network, an impressive personal image, a confident interview, and a timely follow-up.

SUMMARY

Conducting a job search is a demanding and complex process. The key is good planning and effective preparation. Without these two elements, whatever effort is made in the execution will not likely succeed.

Planning is the foundation, and it may be difficult because of the emotional trauma associated with job changing and job loss. Proper planning calls for setting goals and taking an inventory of available resources, including personal networks, job search tools, and interpersonal skills.

Preparation is the translation of plans into a viable program. It includes preparing the résumé and the F-A B, writing various letters, and giving specific attention to communication techniques and skills. This is the time when the job seeker works to develop a success-oriented attitude that accepts nothing less than the best.

Execution is the activation of the planning and preparation into a dynamic and positive job search.

CHAPTER

4

THE TOOLS OF
THE TECHNICAL
JOB SEARCH:
"PAPERWARE"

Much of the activity associated with a technical job search is performed using various "tools." Because many of these tools consist of paper items such as résumés, newspaper advertising, applications, and letters, I have chosen to call them *paperware.*

This chapter will examine the paperware associated with the job search with a view toward making these items work in the technical job seeker's favor. The proper preparation and use of résumés, the résumé alternative, or feature-accomplishment-benefit presentation (F-A-B), the accompanying cover letter, applications for technical positions, follow-up letters, and acceptance letters will be addressed.

Particular emphasis will be given to the misconceptions and misuse of résumés and the pitfalls that can befall the technical job hunter. A special concern is the representation of technical experience and competence in the résumé and how the job candidate can focus relevant experience toward the job being sought. Examples of recommended technical résumé formats are included. The use of action words in technically oriented résumés is discussed, and a list of words is provided (see Figure 4–1).

The concept of the F-A-B presentation is introduced as a preferable alternative to the résumé.

THE RÉSUMÉ: BLESSING OR CURSE?

I am frequently asked by employer clients to "send a résumé." If I have one, I will usually do so because experience has taught me that the résumé is so entrenched in the minds of both job seekers and employers as the primary job search tool that any valid objections I might raise usually fall on deaf ears.

The fact is that the résumé has so many faults that its use in any but a limited role is questionable. But because it is viewed as standard equipment in the job search repertoire, particularly that of the technical candidate, a discussion on the pros and cons of the résumé is appropriate.

FIGURE 4–1. Résumé Action Word Guide

Using the right words or the words that convey the greatest impact is always important, but never more than when preparing a résumé or an F-A-B. Some words convey action and have greater impact than others you might choose. These words tell the reader what you *did*. A word of caution is appropriate: Choose your words carefully! They are representing you. Remember, the following words are only a partial list. Start listening to words and the impressions they make.

1. Accomplished	16. Introduced
2. Achieved	17. Learned
3. Administered	18. Led
4. Analyzed	19. Managed
5. Assisted	20. Organized
6. Conceived	21. Planned
7. Contributed	22. Programmed
8. Created	23. Qualified
9. Delegated	24. Reduced
10. Designed	25. Reorganized
11. Developed	26. Saved
12. Implemented	27. Solved
13. Increased	28. Succeeded
14. Innovated	29. Supervised
15. Installed	

A Definition

A good starting point is to understand what a résumé is and what it is not.

1. A résumé is a marketing tool written from a candidate's perspective.

2. Résumés are written by novices (candidates) who are attempting to present their backgrounds to employers whom they haven't met regarding jobs about which they have little or no information. The term *novice* applies only to résumé-writing ability, not to technical skills. This is based on the fact that technical professionals enter the job market every two to five years on the average. Therefore, their résumé-writing experience is limited.

3. If the employer who reviews the résumé misreads or misunderstands what the candidate is trying to convey, the candidate is not present to defend or correct the false impression.

4. Its accuracy is questionable. Even when the writer makes a special effort to be accurate, the résumé must be viewed as biased because it has been written by someone who is trying to present his or her background in the most favorable manner.

5. It is highly probable that the veracity of résumés is also at issue. Studies have shown that at least a third of all résumés are fraudulent in some respect. This means an outright lie concerning education, work experience, or accomplishments—more than simple bias.

6. A résumé is used more often to screen out candidates than to screen them in. If the reader does not see the right technical buzzwords, the résumé (and the candidate) is passed by.

7. A résumé is prepared by a candidate for a position. This implies that the person is "applying" for the job rather than being "sought out" for the position.

There are valid uses for written documentation concerning the candidate's background, but the résumé is not the document of choice.

Webster's has this definition of a résumé: "A summing up; a summary; specifically a short account of one's career and qualifications prepared typically by a candidate for a position." If this definition were accepted—and practiced—there would be less confusion.

Résumé Fraud

Where résumés are concerned, the truth is often stretched or ignored. Practically every résumé is approximately 10 percent inaccurate. This is not necessarily because of malicious intent, but because of a personal bias in wanting to present oneself in the best perspective combined with intentional errors in the reporting of dates and facts. Because more than 8 million résumés are sent around the United States every business day, fraud is a major concern to employers. Deceptive and fraudulent résumés include everything from phony educational claims to exaggerated work experience. This ranges from honest errors to outright lies. Many companies accept it as part of doing business. The real victim is the candidate who tries to make a truthful representation.

It is estimated that one-third of all résumé claims for higher education are falsified. Unfortunately, this practice is prevalent among the technical disciplines because a degree is often a requirement for a technical job or is viewed with greater importance than for nontechnical positions. Because of this, employers tend to be more wary of technical résumés than of those from other professions.

If this angers you as a technical professional, you are justified. It's bad enough that employers demand résumés as if they were holy writs, but to have them assume that they are probably falsified in some way adds insult to injury.

Insulating Your Résumé Against Suspicion

There are several steps you can take to ensure that your résumé is looked upon as correct and truthful.

1. *Be absolutely certain your résumé is factual.* Double-check that dates are correct, technical terms are precise, and facts are verifiable.

2. *Stick to factual statements that can be quantified.* Avoid ambiguous claims. "Designed numerous components" could mean two components or a thousand. "Involved in leading-edge research" might also appear on the résumé of the janitor who swept the floors.

3. *Attach letters of praise and recommendation.* In reality they might also be fabrications, but people tend to believe what others say about us while they might have doubts about what we say about ourselves.

4. *Include a statement in your résumé such as "Transcripts of educational institutions and professional references available on request."* Don't include copies of transcripts or names of references. A statement that they are available is sufficient. If requested, they can be provided.

Why People Lie on a Résumé

Why do people stretch the truth or lie on a résumé? Sometimes the truth is more unbelievable than the lie. I recall a candidate whose work history had a one-year gap. Rather than stating what he actually did during that year, the candidate chose to extend the ending date of his last job to give the appearance of continuity. When a reference check revealed that the candidate had left a year before he claimed, the prospective employer eliminated him. The truth was that the candidate came from a wealthy family and took a year off and traveled around the world. The truth was unusual, but it would not have kept the candidate from getting the job. When the résumé was later changed, employers responded positively and expressed the desire to be able to do the same thing. Lying can also give the promise of material gain. If stretching the truth on a résumé a bit might result in a higher paying job, the temptation is strong. Don't do it!

Other factors contributing to résumé falsification are fake diplomas available to those willing to pay the price and employers who exaggerate in want ads about jobs. Even when a résumé is truthful, it is suspect because people will naturally omit their weaknesses and failures. Also, sad to say, many prospective employees erroneously believe that they are not likely to get the job they want without lying.

Exaggeration is far more prevalent than the outright lie. While technical résumés might contain exaggerated claims, management and professional employees are more likely to fabricate résumés. Sales and marketing managers often take credit for the work of others. For example, one overly enthusiastic job seeker claimed to have reorganized office procedures when all he had actually done was rearrange the tables and chairs in the office. Then there were the janitor who presented himself as a "sanitary engineer," the garbage man who called himself a "refuse scientist," and the secretary who titled herself an "executive administrator." Such claims are often made on résumés in order to state facts more persuasively; actually, they are nothing but little white lies. Yet it takes an employer only about 30 seconds to get a good or bad impression after reviewing a résumé.

Putting the Résumé into Proper Perspective

We need to examine the résumé and consider it for what it is. It has been ensconced in our culture as almost a sacred icon, and job hunters are continually hit with the request, "Send me a résumé!" Yet we know that in responding we are more likely to be doing employers a disservice than a service. More often than not, it is the easy way out, done to avoid conflict in the misguided hope of successfully getting an interview and possibly a job.

Nearly every book ever written on job hunting or job changing has a section on résumés. In fact, it's often the major thrust of the book. Authors agonize over the importance of the résumé and advise on the type of paper to use, typeface, printed versus typed, and functional versus chronological formats. A wise job seeker would do well to take this advice with a grain of salt, because the résumé is not an event; that is, nothing happens with a résumé. An interview is an event. A job offer is an event. A résumé is paper with information (albeit questionable) on it.

The typical hiring manager scans the résumé quickly. So quickly, according to most observations, the average reading time is 30 seconds or less. Of that 30 seconds, 80 percent is allocated to the first page. If a prospective employee has something to say, it had better be on the first page and it had better be obvious. Thorough résumé readers, and they are in the minority, read résumés closely for reasons that are not in the writers' interest. They look for "knockout" items that screen the candidate out, not in.

The fact that résumés contain exaggerations or outright lies is no secret. Most employers are aware of this, and therefore much of what is said in a résumé might not be believed. If the buzzwords are there, a résumé might serve to keep the applicant in consideration, but the odds are against it. The fact is that the vast majority of résumés will only be skimmed, scrutinized for the wrong reasons, or dismissed out of hand. A résumé will never get a person a job. Only the face-to-face interview will do that.

Reasons for Employers Not to Ask for Résumés

First, there are basically three types of people who comprise the job market. There are those who are unemployed and actively looking. These are the people who are reading the newspapers and actively mailing out résumés. Next are those who are employed but are unhappy for some reason and are also actively looking. Call these the "mentally unemployed." They, too, read newspaper ads and mail résumés. Then, there are working people who are happy in their jobs but are interested in hearing about opportunities and furthering their careers. Types one and two are basically applicants. Type three are candidates. These are stable and competent employees who are not currently on the street looking.

While you may find yourself in any of the three categories, it is best to be in the third. As a happy and working technical professional, you are in a position to objectively evaluate opportunities that come your way. There is certainly no reason why you should not. Saying "no" and staying at your current position is always a viable option. The first two categories have little choice about preparing a résumé or an F-A-B. The third has no reason to and can confidently say to an employer or recruiter, "I'm not actively looking and therefore do not have a current résumé. However, I would be interested in exploring your opportunity. When could we get together?"

Second, if an employer hires someone who has circulated a résumé, the employer's competitors also now have that résumé and can dig into their files the next time they have a need. While this might seem to work in the job seeker's favor, it could also backfire. As a recruiter, I will tell you that if I discover that a job seeker has mailed paper to every place in town, my enthusiasm diminishes. Employers are less likely to invest their recruiting efforts in a person who is a potential candidate in everyone else's files. Hiring someone only to have that person go over to a competitor within a year is a costly and bitter pill.

Finally, studies have shown that a résumé adds about 12 days to the selection process. If you are looking actively for a job, any delay can be costly. An employer who shows an immediate interest is making a positive statement about your value, whereas employers who have (or appear to have) the luxury to accommodate delays may not be as anxious to hire. At least, that's the impression they give.

USING THE RÉSUMÉ TO YOUR ADVANTAGE

The résumé is presumed to be the central focus of the job search. It is held to be the primary tool of employers who are seeking new employees. It is believed to be the ticket that will get the job seeker into the presence of prospective employers and convey his or her qualifications without the necessity of seeing and talking to each one of them.

Unfortunately, for both job seeker and employer, these assumptions about résumés are not true. In our society the résumé is held in far greater esteem than it deserves. In fact, it is more often than not a disservice to those who use it.

If job applicants are going to be asked for résumés, they should know how to prepare and use them to their advantage. The bottom line is that the only valid use of a résumé is to meet the employer. This means that each résumé must be prepared with the employer in mind (not the applicant), and that if an interview is to be granted the employer's attention must be obtained.

The following advice is directed at preparing meaningful résumés (plural) that reach out and say, "Look at my qualifications! They're what you're looking for! Bring me in for an interview!"

BASIC RÉSUMÉ-WRITING RULES

1. *Be simple.* You've got about 20 seconds to get the employer's attention before your résumé gets cast into oblivion, so you'd better write what the employer wants to see. Look at the examples of résumé formats in Figures 4–2 and 4–3. Your résumé must be easy to read, attractively displayed, and simple.

2. *Be specific.* Employers want to know what you did, how you did it, and what benefit was derived from it. If you worked in a technical environment with specific models of equipment, state the equipment and the models and your level of involvement. Use action words. (See the list provided in Figure 4–1.)

3. *Be brief.* Because you have only 20 seconds to get the employer's attention, you must present the most marketable points in your background in a clear, concise manner. This does not mean that your résumé should be limited to 20 seconds' worth of reading, but what you write had better grab the employer and create enough interest that he or she will read the rest of it.

4. *Be accurate.* You would not intentionally include wrong or misleading information, and you must take care that you do not unintentionally include any either. A little extra effort in researching dates, equipment models, acro-

FIGURE 4–2. Example of Chronological Résumé Format

RÉSUMÉ

John Smith
1234 South Street
Los Angeles, CA 90001

(213) 555-1212

PERSONAL:	Age, Marital Status, Number of Children
EDUCATION:	Degree (level and major) 　　School and Date of Graduation 　　(if no degree, technical training)
EXPERIENCE:	**NAME OF CURRENT EMPLOYER** **City, State**
(Dates of Employment)	*TITLE:* Use action verbs, e.g., designed, developed, implemented, etc. Describe equipment/systems used, with model numbers and correct nomenclature. Describe in terms of feature-accomplishment-benefit. Don't use personal pronouns. Use a narrative form. **NAME OF PREVIOUS EMPLOYER** **City, State**
(Dates of Employment)	*TITLE:* (Same as above)
TECHNICAL TRAINING:	List technical training courses and schools.

GENERAL COMMENTS

Use two pages if necessary. Don't use "Career Objective" or "Salary Requirement." Don't include references on the résumé.

---

nyms, or other facts will pay off. Misspellings, wrong model numbers, and other errors make you look bad. Your résumé represents you, and it must be technically precise. If you are inaccurate and careless in the preparation of your résumé, then it is logical to assume that you will exhibit the same traits in your work.

5. *Be critical.* Read your résumé from the employer's perspective. Would you want to find out more about this person? Would you want to schedule an interview? Have a friend read it for you—a real friend who will tell you if it's a bad résumé. When you're looking for a job, the last thing you need is meaningless flattery and no interviews.

FIGURE 4–3. Example of Functional Résumé Format

RÉSUMÉ

Mary Jones
4321 North Avenue
San Francisco, CA 94001

(213) 555-1212

PERSONAL:	Age, Marital Status, Number of Children
EDUCATION:	Degree (level and major) 　　School and Date of Graduation 　　(if no degree, technical training)
EXPERIENCE:	Employers and dates of employment are omitted and experience is expressed in terms of activity, e.g., **RESEARCH, DESIGN, ADMINISTRATIVE,** or **MANAGEMENT.**
	Activities are expressed in terms of *what* was done (features and accomplishments) and the benefits that were achieved.
TECHNICAL TRAINING:	List technical training courses and schools.

GENERAL COMMENTS

A functional résumé is used when a candidate has numerous jobs and doesn't want to appear to be a "jobhopper." It is also advantageous to emphasize and focus on specific skills that might be lost in a chronological résumé.

THE MECHANICS OF RÉSUMÉ PREPARATION

1. The résumé *must* be typed on white 8½- by 11-inch paper. Fancy typesetting is not necessary.

2. "Name," "Address," and "Telephone Number" should be explanatory (see "Résumé Format"). Your name should be the formal use of your name, for example, John J. Jones. A title is not necessary and might even be used to discriminate. For example, "Mrs.," "Miss," or "Ms" could be used in a discriminatory manner if an employer had a preference for single, rather than married, women (or vice versa). The "Ms" designation has a militant feminist connotation for some people, and regardless of your orientation, the job search is not the place to take positions. Nicknames are acceptable if they promote a positive identification. However, if a nickname is likely to raise eyebrows or evoke any other reaction besides association with you, use your formal name. The telephone number you give should be your home phone. The work phone is used only if your present employer is aware of and approves of your job search activities.

3. The "Personal" line is not necessary and not recommended. You are under no obligation to provide any personal information, and in some cases employers have eliminated résumés with personal information as a matter of policy because they feared accusations of discrimination if the applicant were rejected. If you do choose to include a personal line, give only information that is favorable. For example, age only if under 40, marital status only if married or single (never divorced, widowed, or engaged). Number of children is acceptable if the number is three or less. More than that and you run the risk that the employer will view you as contributing to the population explosion. A comment such as "excellent health" can raise the question "Why is this here? Could it be that the candidate has previously been in some other health condition?" Under no circumstances should you include race, religion, weight, height, or any information that could be construed or twisted to discriminate against you.

The only thing that should be of concern to a prospective employer is whether you possess the qualities and abilities to do the job. Remember, the résumé is your sales tool. You prepare it and control what goes into it. It is not a historical biography. Put in it only things that will contribute to your getting the job you want.

I received a résumé from a female candidate with a "Personal" line on it that read, "Age 22, Married, 1 Child, Age 12." I showed the résumé around the office and asked only what the reader's impression might be. Responses varied from smiles to offhand remarks such as "She must have been a swinging 10-year-old!" The real story was that the candidate was referred to me by her husband, who was an employer client. The child was his daughter by a previous marriage.

The candidate was technically very competent, but no one would know that by reading her résumé. They never got past the "Personal" line.

4. "Education" should be placed prior to "Experience" if it is recent and appears to be of greater importance than experience. It should be placed after experience if it is more than ten years old or if the experience is directly applicable to the position you are seeking. If you do not have a degree, do not list more than three and one-half years of school. Doing so invites conjecture as to why you couldn't complete a four year degree program. Your reason may be valid, but you have nothing to gain by causing the employer to speculate with only limited information. If you have a long list of technical courses such as trade schools, military training, or job-related seminars, you may want to limit the "Education" section to college and university experience and include a "Technical Education" section at the end of your résumé.

5. Use the "Résumé Format" (Figures 4–2 and 4–3) and sample résumés (Figures 4–4 through 4–6) to guide you as you prepare your résumé. Do not try and copy them. Rather, endeavor to present the best "you." The "Résumé Action Word Guide" (Figure 4–1) will give you some ideas, but don't let it limit you.

6. Each résumé you send should be tailored to the job for which you are applying. Use your word processor to move applicable experience where it will be read first. If you can express your background in a way that is similar to the way in which the employer has described the position, you stand a greater chance of gaining interest. A caution: Do not copy word for word what the employer says in a want ad or a job description. This is obvious, and it will most certainly be rejected.

7. Don't list references on the résumé. They should appear on the application only if requested. You should prepare a list of professional and personal references to take to interviews. This should include addresses, telephone numbers (work and home), job titles, number of years acquainted, relationships, and any other pertinent information.

FIGURE 4–4. ENTRY LEVEL RÉSUMÉ
(No Experience to Two Years)

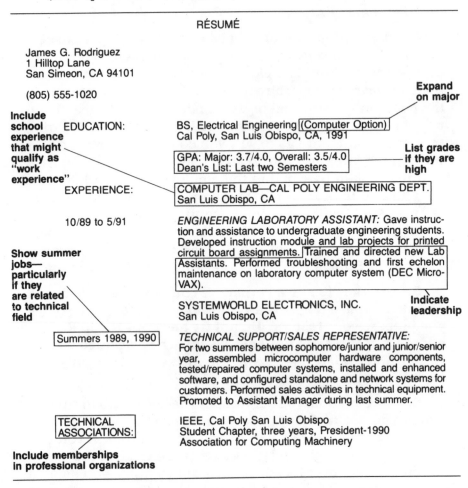

RÉSUMÉ

James G. Rodriguez
1 Hilltop Lane
San Simeon, CA 94101

(805) 555-1020

Expand
on major

Include
school
experience
that might
qualify as
"work
experience"

EDUCATION:

BS, Electrical Engineering (Computer Option)
Cal Poly, San Luis Obispo, CA, 1991

GPA: Major: 3.7/4.0, Overall: 3.5/4.0
Dean's List: Last two Semesters

List grades
if they are
high

EXPERIENCE:

COMPUTER LAB—CAL POLY ENGINEERING DEPT.
San Luis Obispo, CA

10/89 to 5/91

ENGINEERING LABORATORY ASSISTANT: Gave instruction and assistance to undergraduate engineering students. Developed instruction module and lab projects for printed circuit board assignments. Trained and directed new Lab Assistants. Performed troubleshooting and first echelon maintenance on laboratory computer system (DEC Micro-VAX).

Show summer
jobs—
particularly
if they
are related
to technical
field

Indicate
leadership

SYSTEMWORLD ELECTRONICS, INC.
San Luis Obispo, CA

Summers 1989, 1990

TECHNICAL SUPPORT/SALES REPRESENTATIVE:
For two summers between sophomore/junior and junior/senior year, assembled microcomputer hardware components, tested/repaired computer systems, installed and enhanced software, and configured standalone and network systems for customers. Performed sales activities in technical equipment. Promoted to Assistant Manager during last summer.

TECHNICAL
ASSOCIATIONS:

Include memberships
in professional organizations

IEEE, Cal Poly San Luis Obispo
Student Chapter, three years, President-1990
Association for Computing Machinery

8. A brief and to-the-point cover letter should accompany the résumé (see Figure 4–7). Avoid the positive prose about how marvelous you are and how you can contribute to the company. Everybody else says this, and you want the employer to read your letter and go on to read your résumé. Include only a statement of the job for which you are applying and that your résumé is enclosed and contains a clear statement of your qualifications. Unless you are specifically requested to include current salary, omit it. If you are pressed

FIGURE 4–5. Intermediate Résumé (Two to Five Years)

RÉSUMÉ

Susan Lee Chang
333 Harley Hill
Riverside, CA 92777

(714) 555-9988

EDUCATION: BS, Computer Science/Mathematics   **Point out**
University of California, Irvine, CA, 1988   **assignments
involving
independence
and trust**

EXPERIENCE: DESIGNER BRAND GRAPHICS, INC.
Costa Mesa, CA

9/88 to Present   *SCIENTIFIC PROGRAMMER:* Develop specifications, programs, and maintain graphic software for computer-aided design package sold commercially by Designer Brand Graphics. Work independently at customer sites performing modifications and custom designs as per customer specifications. Programming is in C and proprietary 4GL for graphics package. Systems supported are DEC/VAX, NeXT, Apple Macintosh, and IBM PC under OS/2. (12/89 to present)

**Junior and
intermediates
should
show *each*
position
held at a
company**

PROGRAMMER—SUPPORT: Junior member of design team for 3D CAD project. Selected over 7 other programmers. Completed 16-week company training program. Finished at top of class of 10 students. Curriculum included C programming language, 4GL, CAD operations, and structured analysis and design. (9/88 to 11/89)

**List publications
(especially if
experience
is limited)**

TECHNICAL
ASSOCIATIONS:

IEEE, Orange County Chapter
Data Processing Management Association

PUBLICATIONS: "Computerized Designs in Electronic Circuits," *Collegiate Computer Graphics,* January, 1988

TECHNICAL: 2D and 3D computer-aided design,
University of Southern California, one week

**Emphasize
Technical
Training**

---

for a salary expectation, your safest approach is to say, "Salary and compensation are open."

COMMON MISTAKES FOUND ON RÉSUMÉS

1. *Inappropriate length.* This includes trying to expand six months' experience into three pages as well as trying to squeeze 20 years onto one page. Keep in mind that the

FIGURE 4—6. Experienced Résumé (More Than Five Years)

RÉSUMÉ ·

Candice Date
2468 Westshore Drive   **Home**
Santa Barbara, CA 90111   **Phone**

(805) 555-1212

                                            Emphasize
                                            Advanced
EDUCATION: MS, Telecommunications Engineering   **Education**
              UCLA, Los Angeles, CA, 1984

              BS, Business Administration
              Cal State Fullerton, Fullerton, CA, 1981

EXPERIENCE: OPFIBER TELECOMMUNICATIONS, INC.
              Van Nuys, CA

7/86 to Present   *SENIOR SYSTEMS ENGINEER:* Designed and installed a
                  voice and data communications local area network (LAN) in
                  three company plant sites. Project lead over eight Analysts
Feature-   assigned to the project. Developed a data base for customer
Accomplishment accounts and cut previous billing cost by 40% (from $55K/mo.
                  to $33K/mo.)

              Systems environment is DEC VAX/Cluster with (2) IBM 3090/
              MVS/XA. Application programming is in COBOL utilizing the
              DB2 DBMS.

              INTERCITY BANK SERVICES
              Los Angeles, CA   **Ensure**
8/81 to 6/86   **equipment**
                                                        and models
              SENIOR PROGRAMMER/ANALYST: Designed, wrote specifi- **are correct**
              cations, developed, and implemented demand deposit ac-
              counting system using IMS DBMS with DB/DC.

Technical training   Systems used were an IBM 3083 and 4381 under the MVS/XA
should be   operating system. Programming was PL/1 with approximately
emphasized   20% utilizing ALC for on-line modules.

TECHNICAL   IBM Systems School, Advanced DB2, 1987
TRAINING   Netskills Tech, Network Support, 1989
              ProSkills, Technical Leadership, 1990

---

first page is the important page, and unless it can gain and keep interest, the rest won't be read.

2. *Being "cutesy."* Using colored paper, off-size paper, unusual graphics, or any attempt to come across as being different. A bit of flair is sometimes appropriate for someone in art or graphics, or when a demonstration of skills can be presented in a tasteful and acceptable manner; however, there is no way to predict how an employer might react, and it is always safe to be conventional.

FIGURE 4–7. Sample Cover Letter

Donald G. Bladeless
7982 Van Allen Avenue
Sunnytown, CA 90111

(213) 555-3210

February 14, 1991

Mr. William Charleston
Director of Engineering
Pacific Engineering, Inc.
4700 Coastal Parkway
Los Angeles, CA 90200

Dear Mr. Charleston,

As a follow-up to our telephone conversation last Wednesday, I'm enclosing my résumé as you requested. It is formatted in a feature-accomplishment-benefit form to give you a better overview of my qualifications for the position of Research Project Leader in your department.

Bill Marlow at Alpha Aerospace suggested I meet with you concerning your need. I understand you and Bill worked together at Omega Aircraft, and he told me about your project.

I have over ten years' experience in rotary wing design and led the project for the high-speed weapons platform at United Technologies, my current company.

I will call you Tuesday to discuss your requirement. I am also available to meet with you any morning next week. In the meantime, if there is any additional information I might provide or if you have any questions concerning my background, please call. I can be reached during the day at (213) 555-1234, ext. 45 and during the evening at (213) 555-3210.

Sincerely,

Donald G. Bladeless

Enclosure: Résumé

---

3. *Including a picture with the résumé.* This eliminates objectivity, invites discrimination, and is generally seen as narcissistic.

4. *Typographical errors, grammatical errors, erasures, and other indications of carelessness.* The candidate is written off as unprofessional and careless.

5. *Calling the résumé a "curriculum vitae."* This is only done by academic types or health professionals and is not acceptable in the technical or business world.

6. *Falsification of credentials.* This is very serious. In fact, lying on a résumé is grounds for dismissal in many states.

7. *Exaggerated or inflated descriptions of past duties and accomplishments.* Accomplishments should be described in active verbs and expressed in quantitative terms. Bottom-line terms expressing numbers and percentages in dollars will get attention. More important, it is necessary to tell how these accomplishments can benefit a prospective employer.

8. *Accomplishments that aren't accomplishments or that work in reverse.* This includes memberships in mutual admiration societies that anyone can join with the price of admission. Active participation in and support of professional and technical societies are a different matter, and they should definitely be mentioned on a résumé.

9. *A historical or biographical approach that reads more like an obituary than the accomplishments and qualifications of a living person.* A résumé is a representation of a live person that points out the way that person can contribute to the employer's future. An obituary tells only about someone's past.

USING A PROFESSIONAL RÉSUMÉ-WRITING SERVICE

The Yellow Pages and the want ads are full of résumé-writing services. These are people who, for a price, will write your résumé for you and reproduce it in typeset quality on good paper. Their claim is the production of "winning résumés" or "résumés that get jobs." Their appeal is that you don't have to write your own résumé and that their "professional" efforts must be superior to yours.

I do not recommend the use of résumé-writing services, especially for a technical person. I receive several hundred unsolicited résumés each week, and I can spot the professionally prepared ones immediately. They have a sameness about them, and they appear too polished and slick. The prose used often indicates that the writer knew little or nothing about the technical experience being described. Because your résumé is going to a technical manager, you must have precision in your technical descriptions and accomplishments. The professional résumé writers tend to lean toward embellishment and exaggeration rather than hard facts, and this is the opposite of the image that a highly qualified technical professional wants to present. The exception is having someone assist you who is knowledgeable about your technical specialty.

A FINAL WORD ON RÉSUMÉS

The preparation of your résumé is a first step in your search for new career opportunities. Its importance is limited, but it is a part of the total effort, and you want to get maximum benefit from its use. An indirect benefit you will derive from preparing it is that it will help you organize and present your background and qualifications in a concise and orderly fashion. You know yourself better than anyone else, but you will probably have to think a moment to pick out your most significant features. Making the right career move is hard work and one of the most important things you will do in your life. Give it your best shot!

THE FEATURE-ACCOMPLISHMENT-BENEFIT (F-A-B) PRESENTATION

It is necessary for an employer to have information in some form of data sheet format. To be effective, this must be accurate in its representation of facts and meaningful in what it represents to the prospective employer.

An alternative to the résumé that will present your background more effectively is the feature-accomplishment-benefit, or F-A-B presentation. It provides an effective alternative to the résumé. It is unique because it states what the candidate has done (*features*); what the candidate has done with those features (*accomplishments*); and how a prospective employer might benefit as a result of what has been accomplished (*benefits*). It is not a shot in the dark or a guess, but a focused effort directed at a particular employer for a particular job.

When you send your résumé to a prospective employer, you want to stand out from other candidates or applicants. Your goal is to favorably attract the employer's attention so that you will be called in for a face-to-face interview. Unfortunately, résumés generally do not work in your favor. My experience is that approximately one hire results for every 200 résumés sent. This might seem to justify a numbers game—that is, send out 200 résumés and get a job. If you're not particular about where you work, you will probably be successful. Hopefully, your career is more important to you than that.

As a recruiter and employment consultant, I frequently present candidates to employers. If I did no more than send their résumés, I would waste a lot of stamps and time. I would also be doing the candidates a disservice. Flinging paper against a wall in the hope that some of it will stick is a poor way to help someone find a job. Considering the minimal attention given to résumés by employers, I want to improve the odds of attracting a positive look.

My approach is to prepare a candidate background summary or profile. This is a one-page document expressing the candidate's background in terms of the employer's job specification (see Figure 4–8). I am careful to use the terms the employer has used and avoid references to skills or background items that are not related to the job at hand. I usually attach the résumé, but only as a supplement. This focused approach results in more face-to-face interviews and therefore more hires.

FIGURE 4–8. Sample F-A-B (Feature-Accomplishment-Benefit)*

April 5, 1991

BACKGROUND SUMMARY OF: **DONALD G. BLADELESS**

POSITION: **RESEARCH PROJECT LEADER**

Currently the **PROJECT LEADER** for the High-Speed Weapons Platform Project at United Technologies. Have been in this position since the feasibility phase and am about to complete testing and move into implementation. } **Feature**

Led a team of 15 engineers in developing high-speed blade design and transmission redesign. Completed the design and testing phases two months early and at 92% of projected budget. Received three letters of commendation from customer. } **Accomp.**

Currently seeking a new challenge that would permit continued growth in a similar environment. Could bring experience and proven performance to the project at Pacific Engineering. } **Benefit**

Continue with F-A-B by listing items applicable to the prospective employer's environment. This can be done within a résumé structure. This will also include EDUCATION, ASSOCIATIONS, etc., because they represent *features* that can be translated into *accomplishments* that can spell *benefits*.

---

*Also called a *Background Summary.*

    What I call a "candidate background summary" is in reality an F-A-B. It can be used just as effectively by the candidate either as a substitute or a supplement to the résumé.

Purpose of the F-A-B

You want to present your experience, skills, and background in a way that shows how you can be of value to an employer. An F-A-B does the following:

1. It demonstrates how you can benefit the employer.

2. It provides details about what you have done in your career and particularly in your current job.

3. It focuses on the special skills and experiences that are related to the employer's needs.

4. It is totally positive and does not contain any negative or disqualifying information.

Components of the F-A-B

F-A-B is an acronym for "feature-accomplishment-benefit." Let's examine and define each of these three components.

1. *Feature.* A feature is a distinctive quality, a fact, a characteristic, or a specific detail about an entity. In this case the entity is you. What is it about you that you would like a prospective employer to notice? For example, you are an electrical engineer or computer software developer. You have a BS degree in electrical engineering from a well-known university. You have ten years' experience in specific areas in your field. These are facts. They are absolute and objective. They are not subject to opinion or judgment.

2. *Accomplishment.* An accomplishment is something you have done or performed in your career. Accomplishments are historical; that is, they happened in the past. Like features, accomplishments are absolutes, that is, you have either done what you claim or you haven't. Accomplishments are expressed in quantitative terms and may be over time. For example, you designed a new type of printed circuit board for which you hold a patent. You wrote a technical article that was published in a prestigious journal in your industry. You developed a manufacturing process that increased production by 20 percent and profits by 25 percent. When you get into the areas of increased performance and profits, there may be room for some interpretation. However, these are expressions of what you have done.

3. *Benefits*. Benefits are projections of how your features and accomplishments can be of value to a prospective employer. Benefits are referred to in the future tense. They are why an employer would want to hire you. If the manufacturing process you claimed as one of your accomplishments increased production by 20 percent and profit by 25 percent, you could reasonably claim a similar performance in the future.

HOW TO PREPARE YOUR F-A-B

In the discussion on résumé preparation, I emphasized the importance of putting your best effort into the preparation of your résumé. I also stressed that you must do it yourself since no one knows you better. Unlike the résumé, I do not believe the F-A-B is of limited value. Because it focuses on what you can bring to future employers by expressing benefits that they can identify with, it is far more valuable.

A more important advantage of the F-A-B over the résumé is that it is tailored for each employer. A résumé can do this also, but it is generally thought of as a more generic tool. When a résumé is fashioned and focused with a single employer in mind, it tends to resemble the F-A-B.

Steps in Preparing an F-A-B

1. *List your features*. These are the one-, two-, or three-word descriptions of what you are: your job title, education, experience, recognition, or unusual experiences.

2. *List your career history in chronological order*. Include everything—every position and all duties, titles, promotions, superiors, co-workers, training received, accomplishments, and awards, as well as reasons for leaving (and accepting the position) and your likes and dislikes about each position.

This is not for publication, so let yourself go. Write down everything you remember about each aspect of your career.

Be precise and accurate about your accomplishments. Express them in terms of quantitative measurements. Embellish the things you are especially proud of. Put down how you did them and why. Don't worry about being wordy; there will be time for editing later.

This exercise has two purposes. First, it will be the resource from which you will construct your F-A-B. Second, it is a memory jogger. Reaching into your past and drawing out detailed facts about your career history will make each detail fresh in your mind. When asked about some aspect of your work in an interview, it will be on the tip of your tongue. There will be no hesitation or stumbling to remember. This will work to your benefit by giving you a more professional appearance.

3. *Prepare an F-A-B for each potential employer.* For each employer, study your list of features and accomplishments and consider what would be of interest to that employer. Ask yourself what you have done that could be expressed as a benefit.

4. *Organize your F-A-B.* Take a plain piece of paper; a legal size page (8½" × 14") is best. Turn it to the landscape or horizontal position, divide it with vertical lines into three equal sections, and label the first section "Features," the second "Accomplishments," and the third "Benefits." In the left column, under "Features," list a feature you believe would be of interest to the employer you're trying to reach. Next, under "Accomplishments," write down the accomplishments that have resulted from the feature. Now express the "Benefits" the employer would receive if you were hired. Repeat this process for all the appropriate "Features" and "Accomplishments."

5. *If you have a word processor, enter your work and save it.* You can use it later for additional employers.

6. *Read over the F-A-B.* An English professor once told me to "worry about words." He meant that I should examine what I wanted to say or write to see whether there was a more appropriate word I might use or whether there was any chance of being misunderstood or misinterpreted.

7. *Have someone else read it over.* Just as I encouraged you to be critical in résumé preparation, the same holds true for F-A-Bs.

There is a story that Napoleon had a corporal on his staff for the single purpose of reading the communiqués he prepared for his generals. It is said that the corporal was considered to be the stupidest man in Napoleon's army, and Napoleon believed that if he could understand what was written, then surely the generals would understand.

This is not meant to imply that employers are stupid; rather, it is a plea for simple and easily understood writing. I receive résumés and letters from thousands of job hunters. Most of them get minimum attention, and I admit that I am probably missing some very qualified people. However, what attracts my eye is clearly stated facts (features), related experiences (accomplishments), and straightforward statements of what I want to hear (benefits).

Often job seekers call me as a follow-up to sending a résumé, and when I tell them I didn't see any of the things on their résumés that my clients might be interested in, they say "Yes, but I can do. . . . " My reply is, "Why didn't you put that on your résumé?" The standard answer is, "I didn't know you were looking for that!" I will state this in italic type so you won't miss it: *It is the job seeker's responsibility to find out what the employer wants and direct the presentation accordingly.*

Memory Joggers for Preparing Your F-A-B

When I critique a résumé or an F-A-B with a job candidate, I frequently hear "I didn't think that event was important!" It may or may not be important. The problem is *who* didn't think it was important. Résumés and F-A-Bs are not written for the benefit of the candidate; they are written for prospective employers. You must write from the employer's point of view, expressing your features, accomplishments, and benefits so that the employer will want to meet you.

The best way to present yourself is through examples and illustrations. Listing features, accomplishments, and benefits is easier if you think of specific instances instead of a generalized list. The following are some specifics you might consider:

1. *Contribution to the "bottom line."* Did you do anything for previous or current employers to make or save money? How did you do it? Was it a sales contribution? A new or improved process? What was the occasion? Provide a basis for comparison. Express it in actual dollar amounts. Use percentages for comparisons.

2. *Creation of new products, processes, or ideas.* Did you invent, develop, or design something that is unique or might be of value if you did the same thing for a new employer? You may have identified a problem and/or proposed a solution. Even if the problem or the solution isn't relevant, it shows that you have the ability to function as a problem solver and troubleshooter.

3. *Administrative skills.* Did you hold a management or supervisory position? What administrative skills have you demonstrated? Were you promoted? Were there special conditions such as being selected over several competitors or being very junior in the company (a rising star)? Many people believe the stereotype that technical people have no administrative or managerial skills or that they do not desire that type of work. Stating your abilities will dispel that view.

4. *Communication skills.* Have you written any technical (or nontechnical) material? Have you performed any training—formal or informal? Have you attended communication seminars or workshops? Do you have public speaking or negotiation skills? Use specific examples.

5. *Contributions to employers.* State examples of noteworthy work you have done for your current and past employers. Especially list policy and goal-setting roles you have played. Did you approach your job in some unique manner? Did you change the structure of your job to make

it more productive or easier? Did you have additional duties besides your assigned job? Were they voluntary? Did you receive recognition for the extra work?

Express your accomplishments in a narrative or anecdotal form. Everybody loves a story. For example, if you designed a machine part, instead of simply stating the fact, consider something like the following:

> Designed a camshaft for a widget. A client required a special design not currently available and I volunteered to perform the design work. The part was produced a full two weeks prior to the customer's request date and the customer wrote me a letter of appreciation.

Examples used in your F-A-B should be quantified and stated in a comparative context when possible. "Increased sales significantly" means very little, while "Increased annual sales by 35 percent over previous year's sales" provides a comparison that makes your accomplishment meaningful.

WHAT AN F-A-B WILL DO FOR YOU

1. *An F-A-B can take the place of a résumé as a marketing tool.* You are trying to present yourself to prospective employers in a way that will move them to grant you a face-to-face interview. Unlike the résumé, which tends to be more structured, the F-A-B can be formatted to be more appealing.

2. *Because the F-A-B is not a résumé, it will make you appear unique to prospective employers.* In the competition for recognition, a high-quality F-A-B will stand apart from a pile of résumés.

3. *An F-A-B is logical, organized, thoughtful, and effective.* It is an expression of the most meaningful aspects of your background, oriented especially for a potential employer.

4. *Preparing the F-A-B is an excellent exercise in preparation for a job-winning interview.* Putting it together forces you to think about yourself and your strengths from a feature, accomplishment, and benefit point-of-view.

A FINAL WORD ON F-A-Bs

The F-A-B is a marketing tool. It is used to sell your skills and background to prospective employers. You may determine that it is not appropriate for a particular situation, and that will not hurt my feelings. You know yourself better than anyone. The decision to use a résumé format or an F-A-B is up to you. My advice is to try both approaches and see which works best.

THE JOB APPLICATION

While the résumé and the F-A-B are candidate tools, the job application form belongs to the employer. There are restrictions about questions that can be asked stemming from EEO laws and regulations, but the structure generally favors the employer. Employers normally take the job application form seriously, and you should also. Treating it casually or being careless in completing it is a sure way to make a poor first impression. More than likely, you will be disqualified from further consideration.

The job application form has the apparent objective of gathering candidate history to determine background and qualifications for a position. This is certainly the case, but it also can provide a wealth of other information about the candidate's attitude and personal characteristics.

Ideally, the job application form should be easy to read and understand, be in compliance with current EEO laws, be visually pleasing, and not contain any misleading or confusing questions. Unfortunately, few even come close. What one person says or writes, another will misinterpret. Because the author is not present with an interpretive explanation, you will be left to answer the questions as best as you can. Most questions are straightforward, but some can be misleading. Some might even be offensive. You should keep in mind that offense was not intended, and reply accordingly.

Some of the subjective information employers might get from reviewing how you complete their job application forms includes the following:

1. *Your attitude toward the form.* If you misspell words, print illegibly, omit items, or provide inadequate information, it will appear that the form is not important to you.

2. *Your communication skills.* The ability to express yourself clearly in written communications is a valuable asset. Clear and concise expressions will tell the employer that you understand what is being asked and that you want your background and experience stated clearly.

3. *Your attitude toward references.* The references you list may be revealing. If the only references you provide are contemporaries or personal friends, the employer may infer there is a reason for not listing former managers and/or clients.

If possible, request the job application form prior to going to your face-to-face interview. This will save you time when you report for your interview, and it will preclude your being rushed to complete it. The more you are rushed, the more likely it is that you will make spelling errors, miss items, make mistakes that cause the form to look messy, and include conflicting or erroneous information.

Having the job application form beforehand allows you to complete it at your leisure. I recommend that you type, rather than print, your responses. I also recommend that you write out your responses on a separate sheet before placing the final draft on the form. This way, you will be able to proofread it thoroughly and put your best foot forward.

Checking for Consistency with Your Résumé

You must be sure that the facts and figures you give on the job application form are consistent with the information on your résumé or F-A-B. An omission or inconsistency could cause an employer to view you with suspicion even though it was perfectly innocent. Here are some items to consider:

1. *Numbers.* Make sure that dates, total months, percentages, and dollars agree.

2. *Job information.* Job titles, duties, names of supervisors, equipment, company name, and location should coincide.

3. *Facts.* Education (schools, majors, honors), personal data, extracurricular activities, and the like should be consistent.

4. *Communication skills.* Does the narrative description project your writing and communication skills favorably? Be careful not to convey opinions or bias. Remain objective.

5. *Career objectives.* What you write about past jobs should indicate growth and a movement toward improvement in skills, job responsibility, and education.

If there is an area about which you are uncertain, call the employer's human resources representative for clarification. If it is still unclear, answer it as briefly and to the point as possible.

CORRESPONDENCE USED IN THE JOB SEARCH

You will write many letters in the course of your job search. It goes without saying that they should be neatly constructed, intelligently written, appropriately organized, free of grammatical and spelling errors, and directed to the right person.

You will write several types of letters, and each type will be discussed here. Most advice regarding job searches is directed to the mechanics of writing résumés. Just as the résumé must be precise and targeted, so must the letters you write.

In the discussion on preparing the résumé and the F-A-B, I stressed the importance of correct spelling, good grammar, and direct, to-the-point writing. Résumés may only be scanned, but it is certain that your correspondence will be read. Cover and broadcast letters may be approached more casually, but other letters are likely to be read in their entirety.

My experience with technical people has shown me that they tend to concern themselves less with communication skills than do people from other disciplines. This is a generalization, and there are many technical people who write and speak as well as anyone else. However, writing skills are normally not considered a primary subject of technical education curriculums.

Good communication skills are an asset in every facet of your life. If you are the best at your technical discipline, the ability to communicate well will only enhance your effectiveness. The letter you attach to your résumé or F-A-B is the first impression a prospective employer will have of you. If it is sloppy, full of errors, and rambling, you may be certain the employer will not say, "Oh well, this is such a great [whatever], we'll overlook the bad cover letter." Communicate well and that's how you'll be perceived—from a technical perspective and otherwise. An excellent reference for the usage and mechanics of cover letters is *The Perfect Cover Letter*, by Richard H. Beatty (Wiley, 1989).

Among the "paperware" tools available to the technical job seeker are several types of letters, including the following:

- Cover letters
- Broadcast letters
- Thank-you letters
- Follow-up letters
- Networking letters
- Acceptance letters
- Rejection letters

Letters have a special significance to the technical candidate because they must convey technical competence as well as serve as transmittal documents for résumés and F-A-Bs. Your goal in using a letter in your job search is to:

1. Present your technical competence to prospective employers in a personal context.

2. Provide an introduction for your résumé or F-A-B.

3. Formally introduce yourself to prospective employers, express thanks, follow up on interviews, communicate within a network, and accept a position.

4. Motivate prospective employers to want to meet you and find out more about you.

General Rules for Job Search Letters

1. *Follow an established format.* A sample format is shown in Figure 4–9. The layout of letters must be neat and attractive.

2. *Watch out for misspelled words and improper grammar.* Access to PC-based word processors and their integrated spellcheckers makes misspelled words inexcusable. Misspellings and poor grammatical construction come across to the reader as carelessness, ignorance, or incompetence.

3. *Project a professional appearance.* Use personal stationery. Do not use company stationery unless it is your company. Using the supplies of your current employer makes you appear either cheap or a thief. Never conduct any part of your job search on your present employer's nickel.

4. *Address the letter to a specific individual by name.* Avoid sending it to a title such as "Director of Engineering." Never send it to the personnel department. It is difficult enough to get a technical manager to notice your letter. If personnel gets it, you may be assured it will receive little or no attention. Personnel representatives, while well-meaning, are seldom skilled in technical requirements. They are certainly not as motivated to fill positions as the technical manager is.

FIGURE 4–9. Job Search Letter Format

Personal Stationery Heading —

Donald G. Bladeless
7982 Van Allen Avenue
Sunnytown, CA 90111

(213) 555-3210

February 14, 1991 — *Date letter sent*

Mr. William Charleston — *Name of hiring authority*
Director of Engineering — *Hiring authority's title*
Pacific Engineering, Inc. — *Company name*
4700 Coastal Parkway — *Company street address*
Los Angeles, CA 90200 — *Company city, state, ZIP*

Dear Mr. Charleston, — *Salutation*

BODY OF LETTER xxxxx xxxxx xxxxx xxxxx xxx xxxxx
xxxxxxx xxxxxx xxxxx xxxxxx. xxx xxxxxx xxxxxxx xxxxxxx
xxxxx xxxxx xxxx xxxx xxxxx xxxx xxxxxxx xxxx xxxxxx
xxxxxxx xxxxxx xxxxx xxxxxx. xxx xxxxxx xxxxxxx xxxxxxx
xxxxx xxxxx xxxx xxxx xxxxx xxxx xxxxxxx xxxx xxxxxx

xxxxxxx xxxxxx xxxxx xxxxxx. xxx xxxxxx xxxxxxx xxxxxxx
xxxxx xxxxx xxxx xxxx xxxxx xxxx xxxxxxx xxxx xxxxxx
xxxxxxx xxxxxx xxxxx xxxxxx. xxx xxxxxx xxxxxxx xxxxxxx
xxxxx xxxxx xxxx xxxx xxxxx xxxx xxxxxxx xxxx xxxxxx

xxxxxxx xxxxxx xxxxx xxxxxx. xxx xxxxxx xxxxxxx xxxxxxx
xxxxx xxxxx xxxx xxxx xxxxx xxxx xxxxxxx xxxx xxxxxx
xxxx xxxxxx xx xxxxxx xxxx xxxxx

Sincerely, — *Closing*

Signature

Donald G. Bladeless — *Typed name*

Enclosure: Résumé — *Enclosures*

The Cover Letter

The cover letter is what it sounds like. It "covers" the résumé or F-A-B, introducing those tools to prospective employers. It also personalizes them.

A cover letter is focused and directed at a specific person.

Unlike the broadcast letter, it is personal and specific in both direction and message. An example of a cover letter is shown in Figure 4–7.

In a cover letter you address yourself to the employer in a nearly conversational tone. As in any conversation, your goal is to gain the attention of the other person and communicate your message. Because communication is a two-way activity (sending and receiving), you must take great care to ensure that your message is received and understood. The most effective means of getting your message across is to project yourself into the position of the receiver and accurately perceive what the receiver's motivations are. You should consider the following points.

1. *What the employer is looking for.* If you are aware that the employer is looking for technical skills, that is what you want to project. People are not motivated by what *we* want. They are turned on by *their* wants.

2. *What the technical level is of the person to whom you are addressing the letter.* You want to reach the technical manager who can make the decision to hire you. However, this is not always possible. If you're answering an ad, you may be channeled into the personnel department. You can find this out by calling the company and asking the position of the person listed in the ad. If it's personnel, ask for the name of the person managing the technical area where you want to work.

A first-line technical manager is going to be as close to the technology as any hiring authority, so you can show off your technical vocabulary. Consider your current job and what people working at various levels are interested in. A first-line supervisor of only nonmanagement people will be interested in your level of technical ability. A more senior manager may want to know how well you can organize and get along with people.

3. *What personal (nontechnical) factors will motivate the hiring manager to bring you in for an interview.* The more you know about the person you want to communicate with, the more effective your communication will be. If you know someone who works at the company, that person may be able to give you some insight on the personal as well as the technical side. I knew a computer programmer who mentioned to the hiring manager that he was a pitcher on a championship softball team. From then on, his technical ability was secondary. Although this is not the best criterion for being hired, it's close to how hires are made in the so-called "real world."

4. *The company or organization to which you are applying and the industry within which it operates.* If the company is large, you can research its history, organization, and financial position at a library with a good business section. You can obtain company product literature and an annual report just for the asking. It might even be worth your time to stop by the company and pick up the literature personally. It will give you a look at the physical facilities, and you may be able to observe the attitudes of the people who work there.

A smaller company may be more difficult to find out about. Since it's likely your technical expertise is in the area in which the company is working, you will probably know someone who has information about the company. They may even be able to put you in touch with someone at the company who can tell you about the company or assist you in making contact.

The Broadcast Letter

The broadcast letter is a form of cover letter. The difference is that it is mailed to a larger audience—it is "broadcast." You may choose to contact a number of companies in a specific industry or area, and time constraints preclude researching and directing your letter to an individual. I must say that this is not the preferred method, but sometimes it works. The letter should be directed to a title (e.g., "Director of Engineering") if the name of the person holding the position is not available.

Broadcast letters may be used when answering classified

ads if the name of the person trying to fill the position is not known. Want ads frequently request that inquiries be sent to a personnel or human resources representative. Letters concerning employment should always be sent to what is called the "hiring authority." This is the technical manager for whom you will work if you are hired. If the personnel office is the clearing point, your letter will be routed to it. The problem with sending an inquiry about open positions to personnel is the risk that it will be screened against a list of buzzwords or requirements by a nontechnical screener and disqualified. Personnel specialists will tell you this doesn't happen, but I maintain that it does, and far too often for you to take the risk.

Although a broadcast letter is sent to a title rather than a name, it should never give the appearance of being mass produced. I receive a steady stream of letters that start out "Dear Recruiter," and, frankly, I'm turned off. They are generally photocopied, and I get the feeling I am one out of thousands that received the letter. Even if I were interested, I would feel that I'm just a spot on the wall that all these letters and résumés were being thrown against. Rather than starting with "Dear (Whatever)," I recommend "To the Director of Engineering" or "To the Hiring Manager Seeking a Senior Aeronautical Engineer." A sample broadcast letter is shown in Figure 4–10.

Thank-You Letters

Thank-you letters are sent following an interview or employer-initiated activity. It is a courtesy that you should not overlook, even if you do not intend to pursue a job with the employer. Since 95 percent of all job interviewees do *not* send thank-you letters, the mere fact that you send one will make you stand out.

A sample thank-you letter is shown in Figure 4–11. Your object is to extend a courteous "thank you" and restate your interest in the job. Also express a desire to hear from the employer and state your intent to get in touch with your contact person to keep yourself informed so that you can make informed decisions regarding your job search.

FIGURE 4–10. Sample Broadcast Letter

Donald G. Bladeless
7982 Van Allen Avenue
Sunnytown, CA 90111

(213) 555-3210

April 1, 1991

Director of Engineering
Pacific Engineering, Inc.
4700 Coastal Parkway
Los Angeles, CA 90200

To the Director of Engineering:

This is an inquiry concerning your requirement for a senior aeronautical engineer.

A résumé detailing my background is enclosed. It is formatted in a feature-accomplishment-benefit form to give you a better overview of my qualifications.

I have over ten years' experience in jet engine design and am currently a member of the project team developing the minimum signature powerplants for the new generation of stealth attack aircraft.

Aviation Week and Space Technology's article last month concerning Pacific Engineering's research in vectored thrust powerplants was of great interest to me. The opening for the senior aeronautical engineer on the project appears to be a position in which my background and experience could make a definite contribution.

My current project is nearing completion, and I am in the process of evaluating new challenges.

My availability for interviewing is open. Please contact me if additional information is desired. My home phone is (213) 555-3210.

Sincerely,

Donald G. Bladeless

Enclosure: Résumé

FIGURE 4–11. Sample Thank-You Letter
(Following the First Interview)

Donald G. Bladeless
7982 Van Allen Avenue
Sunnytown, CA 90111

(213) 555-3210

March 1, 1991

Mr. William Charleston
Director of Engineering
Pacific Engineering, Inc.
4700 Coastal Parkway
Los Angeles, CA 90200

Dear Bill,

Thank you for the opportunity to meet last Thursday and discuss the position of research project leader in your department.

When we parted, I told you I was interested in the position. I want to reaffirm that interest and add that I have given considerable thought to the contribution I could make to the project.

If there is any additional information you might desire or if there are any questions I might answer, please call.

Again, thank you, Bill. I look forward to a productive and challenging relationship.

Sincerely,

Don Bladeless

GENERAL COMMENTS

The thank-you letter should be warm, personal, low key, short, and to the point. If a first name relationship was established during the interview, use the first name in the letter. A basic rule of getting job offers is to *ask for the job!* This letter is the place to do just that.

The Follow-Up Letter

The follow-up letter is a form of activity that you generate between the time you first interview for a job and the time when you are offered a position or rejected. The time gap between the first interview and the offer can be agonizing. You may receive some offers on the spot, but it is unlikely. It is typical for larger companies to take longer to take action than smaller companies. It probably has something to do with the bureaucratic nature of larger companies, which should cause you to consider whether that is the type of environment in which you want to work.

When you complete an employment interview and the interviewer doesn't tell you when you should expect to hear from the employer, you must ask. The response will tell you much about the person and the company. If the person promises to get back to you the next day and then does it, he or she is to be commended. It may seem strange to make a big deal about people doing what they say they will do, but so many do not that those who do deserve positive recognition. If the employer merely promises to get in touch, you should ask for a date. You can respond with something like "I will look forward to your call. If possible, could you try and get back with me by [approximately one week] so I can plan accordingly? Thank you."

If you do not hear when promised, or if one week has passed, you should send a follow-up letter. You will also want to make a follow-up call, and that will be discussed in Chapter 6.

The follow-up letter is a "dunning" letter. You want to know where the employer is in the decision process, whether or not you are going to receive an offer, and why you haven't been called as promised. You are probably indignant and upset. Of course, your letter will not convey any anger or hostility. Any letter or call during the follow-up period must be carefully considered. You must be creative in your reasons for communicating. After all, didn't the employer tell you the company would be in touch? Following are some suggestions for creative reasons for writing:

1. You wish to expand on the technical experience that is pertinent to the position.

2. You have a work sample that would interest the hiring manager.

3. You have additional references.

4. There is information requested in the job application that you wish to add to or provide.

5. You received or expect to receive another job offer. Be careful with this one. Express it something like the following:

> I want to let you know I am [interviewing with, have received an offer from XYZ or another company]. While this is an excellent opportunity, I would not want to miss being considered by [your company]. If I am being actively considered, I would be pleased, but I would like to know as soon as possible so I can make my plans accordingly.

You must take care that you do not place the employer in an awkward position. It is wise to leave a way out. A suggestion is to use words such as "I know there are many factors you must consider before adding to your staff, but felt you would appreciate my input. Please call if there is any additional information I might provide."

6. Let the employer know you are still interested. You can even express it in the context of a current article about the company (positive, of course) or a positive comment from someone outside the company.

The follow-up letter can be used to reinforce the follow-up call. If the employer gives you another date during the call, put it in writing with an expression of thanks for spending time on the phone with you, restating the time, and expressing anticipation. A sample follow-up letter is shown in Figure 4–12.

FIGURE 4-12. Sample Follow-Up Letter
(When You Haven't Heard from the Employer)

Donald G. Bladeless
7982 Van Allen Avenue
Sunnytown, CA 90111

(213) 555-3210

March 21, 1991

Mr. William Charleston
Director of Engineering
Pacific Engineering, Inc.
4700 Coastal Parkway
Los Angeles, CA 90200

Dear Bill,

Following our meeting three weeks ago concerning the position of
research project leader, you mentioned that you wanted to fill the
position by mid-March.

My personal situation has changed somewhat, and I want to bring you
up to date so that you will have that information to factor into your
plans. My current project is winding down and a new design project
team is being formed to prepare a proposal for the tilt-rotor attack
platform. I have not yet been offered the team lead, but my manager has
asked me to prepare a list of milestones and begin working with the
budget people.

Bill, my first choice would be your project, but I don't want to lose the
opportunity at my current company.

I can appreciate delays in planning because I've been there myself.
However, I don't want timing to be the cause of our not being able to get
together. If you can update me on any plans you might have, I can plan
accordingly.

Bill, I apologize for being aggressive about this matter, but I'm very
interested in the position and aggressiveness is a desirable quality in a
project leader.

Sincerely,

Don Bladeless

The Networking Letter

Networking is the most powerful and effective element in the job hunting equation. More people find jobs and more hires are made through the process of personal contacts than through any other source.

The networking letter is a tool you can use to build your personal job search network. Some of the people you will want to include in your mailing are the following:

1. *Friends and relatives.* Most lists of networking contacts place friends and relatives last. Often these people are the last to know you are actively looking. If you are currently working and merely exploring new possibilities, you may wish to exclude them. However, if you are unemployed, there is no disgrace in looking for honest work. You want to use every avenue.

2. *Former employers.* It's likely that you left your previous employers under positive circumstances. Even if you didn't, there are many people who worked for your previous employers who have gone elsewhere and who have positive feelings for you. Call on them for help.

3. *Former associates.* People who have worked with you know your likes and dislikes and have similar technical backgrounds.

4. *Current associates.* If you don't want your current employer to know you are looking, skip this one except for those you can trust.

5. *Business contacts.* These are people you have met in the course of your profession. Included are sales representatives, vendor technical representatives, and customers.

6. *Professional organizations.* These are the mutual admiration societies that you've paid dues to for years. Let the membership know you are looking, and enlist their help.

This is a generalized broadcast-type letter that (a) tells that you are looking for a change, and (b) asks for assistance and referrals in finding a position. Because you are asking for help, your tone should be friendly and nonthreatening (i.e., giving no implication that you expect a favor returned, etc.). An example of a networking letter is shown in Figure 4–13.

FIGURE 4–13. Sample Networking Letter (Letting People Know You're Looking)

Donald G. Bladeless
7982 Van Allen Avenue
Sunnytown, CA 90111

(213) 555-3210

March 21, 1991

Mr. Tom Franklin
Rocky Mountain Engineering, Inc.
8650 Foothill Lane
San Bernadino, CA 92345

Dear Tom,

Just a short note to let you know I'm considering looking for a new professional opportunity.

I've been working as a research engineer at Alpha Aircraft for the past four years. We're currently wrapping up a project, and I'm taking the opportunity to consider new positions.

Tom, if you are aware of any open positions or know someone who might be interested in my background and experience, please give me a call. My home phone is (213) 555-3210 and my office phone is (213) 555-1234.

Thank you, Tom, for any assistance you might be able to give me. I won't stand on ceremony and will probably be giving you a call. I'll look forward to seeing you at the User's Conference next month.

Sincerely,

Don Bladeless

The Acceptance Letter

This is the letter you send when you have received and accepted an offer of employment. It is generally straightforward, but there are several elements you will want to include.

1. *Acknowledgment.* State that you have received the letter and acknowledge its purpose.

   I have received your letter of [date] offering me the position of [title] with [company].

2. *Thank you and acceptance.* A thank you is always in order. Express your pleasure in accepting the position.

   Thank you for your offer and the courtesies you have extended me. I accept your offer and look forward to joining [company] in the position of [title].

3. *Playback of terms and conditions of employment.* This is probably the most important part of the letter. Many people are so anxious to find a job that they simply call and accept or write their acceptance on the bottom of the offer letter and return it. Many employers even ask prospective employees to do this. It is important that you understand the terms and conditions of your employment. You should restate the salary, your manager's name and title, the start date, and any special conditions discussed during the interview process and prior to the offer.

   It is my understanding that my title [or pay grade] will be [title/pay grade] and that my starting salary will be [amount] per [period—week, month, year]. The first day of employment is [date]. I will be reporting to [name], who is [title]. [*An exception to this would be if the acceptance letter were addressed to the person who hired you.*] As we discussed, I had a family vacation planned for August of this year, and although I do not have vacation time coming, I will be permitted to take this time off without pay.

   Also discuss any other items of importance.

4. *Wrap-up.* End the letter on a positive note and express your thanks again.

Again, thank you for this opportunity. I look forward to being a part of [company].

An example of an acceptance letter is shown in Figure 4–14.

The Rejection Letter

The rejection letter is a necessary piece of business when you must turn down a job offer. A sample rejection letter is shown in Figure 4–15. The usual amenities are addressed and the words of rejection are delivered as softly as possible. An important element is the effort to keep the door open for future opportunities. A rejection is unpleasant, and it is critical that no possibility for future business be eliminated.

SUMMARY

There are few human activities that are performed without the use of tools, and the job search is no exception. Success in any endeavor is enhanced through the employment of good tools and skill in using them.

Paperware tools include the résumé and the F-A-B (Feature-Accomplishment-Benefit presentation) or candidate background summary. Correspondence paperware includes cover letters, broadcast letters, thank-you letters, follow-up letters, networking letters, acceptance letters, and rejection letters.

Although the résumé is considered by most employers and job seekers to be the primary job hunting tool, it has serious problems. Because it is prepared by applicants and candidates, it is biased and of questionable value. However, since it is viewed with such prestige in the employment marketplace, the wise job hunter will take care in the preparation and use of his or her résumé, ensuring that every advantage is utilized.

As an alternative to the résumé, the F-A-B or candidate

FIGURE 4—14. Sample Acceptance Letter

Donald G. Bladeless
7982 Van Allen Avenue
Sunnytown, CA 90111

(213) 555-3210

April 5, 1991

Mr. William Charleston
Director of Engineering
Pacific Engineering, Inc.
4700 Coastal Parkway
Los Angeles, CA 90200

Dear Bill,

I am in receipt of your letter of March 30 offering me the position of research project leader in the Research and Development Department of Pacific Engineering, Inc.

Thank you for the offer of this position and the courtesies extended to me by you and your staff. I am pleased to accept your offer and look forward to joining your team.

It is my understanding that my title will be Senior Engineering Consultant at an annual salary of $57,000. It's also my understanding that my job will be project leader of the research team reporting to you.

Your letter stated that my start date would be April 20. This is fine, and I look forward to starting. As we discussed, I had planned a family vacation during the first two weeks of August and, although I do not have vacation time coming, as we agreed I will be permitted to take this time off without pay.

Again, Bill, thank you for this opportunity. I look forward to being a part of Pacific Engineering. If there is anything I can do prior to my start day, please let me know.

Sincerely,

Don Bladeless

FIGURE 4—15. Sample Rejection Letter

Donald G. Bladeless
7982 Van Allen Avenue
Sunnytown, CA 90111

(213) 555-3210

April 5, 1991

Mr. William Charleston
Director of Engineering
Pacific Engineering, Inc.
4700 Coastal Parkway
Los Angeles, CA 90200

Dear Bill,

I am in receipt of your letter of March 30 offering me the position of research project leader in the Research and Development Department of Pacific Engineering, Inc.

Thank you for the offer of this position and the courtesies extended to me by you and your staff. I have given serious consideration to your offer and must decline.

Bill, I want to thank you for considering me. Pacific Engineering is a fine company and my decision not to take the offer was due to personal circumstances. I particularly appreciate your efforts, and it was a pleasure meeting you and getting to know you.

Again, Bill, thank you. Although I am not able to accept this opportunity, I do not want to close any doors. Please keep me in mind for future opportunities.

Sincerely,

Don Bladeless

---

background summary is a refreshing change of pace. It creates a tool that is custom tailored for each employment opportunity.

The tools of the job search are useful, but they are not the primary ingredient of job search success. *You* are that ingredient. No employer will hire you on the basis of your résumé, F-A-B, or a letter. What these tools *will* do is enhance the person that is you. Because the tools serve as a reflection of you, they should represent you in the most positive manner possible.

5

THE TOOLS OF THE TECHNICAL JOB SEARCH: "HARDWARE"

Until recently, the only tools available to the job seeker were traditional "paperware" tools such as the résumé and various letters. Now, however, technology has given those looking for a career or job change a virtual arsenal that can be brought to bear on the job search. One caveat that must be emphasized is that this hardware cannot find you a job. It can only support your efforts. Only you can perform the task of finding the right position.

As a technical professional looking for a change, it is likely you will have greater access to and knowledge of many of these tools than job hunters in nontechnical disciplines. However, many of the tools are commonplace, and the discussion will focus on their basic and creative uses in the job search.

THE TELEPHONE

The telephone is such a part of our lives that we tend to take it for granted and not think of it as having special significance in a job search situation. However, the telephone is the single most significant and useful piece of hardware available for the job hunter. We use the telephone as if it were an extension of ourselves for nearly everything. Is there any difference when it's used for a job search? The answer is that we use it so casually that we think we know everything about it and fail to maximize its use.

When I first began to work as a recruiter, I was fortunate to receive a thorough grounding in the proper use of the telephone. My initial response to the training was that I had been using telephones all my life and there was nothing new to learn about their use. How wrong I was! The telephone is like any other tool. You can use it casually or you can learn how to use it like a professional. My training taught me how to plan for maximum effectiveness, what to say to elicit the best response, and how to get commitment from the person at the other end of the telephone line.

Types of Telephones and Their Features

A visit to any electronics store will give you a mindboggling education on the variety of telephones available. The common variety with no special features will do for home use, but for your job search there are some features that will be valuable.

Multiline Telephone

If you have more than one line in your home, you should have at least a two-line telephone. If you have other family members (especially teenagers), you already know this. You can't afford to have your phone tied up while a possible job source is trying to contact you. This may seem to be overdoing it; you may feel that if someone "really" wanted to reach you, they would keep trying. Don't believe it! After several unsuccessful tries, the caller will go on to other calls (usually the next most qualified candidate).

People have strange notions when it comes to the telephone. For example, I have met people who believe that if the phone isn't answered the callee isn't interested in receiving the call. This is especially true when there is a job in the offing. I knew a man who considered a busy signal a sign of rudeness. When people call, they expect an answer or, at the minimum, some sort of positive response.

The multiline telephone helps keep the telephone from being tied up. It is likely that at least one of the lines will be free. A suggestion is to use the second line for outgoing calls and for the other family members' incoming calls and leave the line and number you are using in your job search as free as possible.

Call Waiting and Call Forwarding

The Call Waiting feature is aggravating to me. I don't like the irritating "beep-beep" that interrupts my conversations, and I find that the timing of the interruption is always bad. On the other hand, a slight inconvenience and a polite, "Excuse me while I see who's calling," are preferable to the potential consequences of not receiving an important call.

Call Forwarding allows you to have your calls transferred to a phone where you can be reached. This enables you to leave but still give the appearance of availability. Calls can also be forwarded to an answering service or message phone.

Speaker Phone

Speaker phones are another irritant to me. On the surface, they seem like useful devices. They allow you to work with your hands free. There's no wrestling with a receiver or developing a crick in your neck from balancing the handset on your shoulder. However, to the listener it sounds as if you're talking from the bottom of a well. It also sounds arrogant and condescending, with a definite lack of privacy. If you wish to work hands-free and feel that the standard handset is an impediment, there are headsets and microphones available at nominal costs. These are used by telephone operators and telemarketing people. Unless you're on the phone a great deal, my advice is to use the standard setup.

Message Phone

The message phone, or answering machine, is extremely valuable to the job seeker. Technical people are usually working in an environment where answering the telephone can be distracting, an inconvenience, or even impossible. I recall a computer hardware design manager who wished to extend an offer to a hardware design engineer whom I was representing in a search. He preferred to extend the offer himself and finally called me in frustration after he had tried to reach the candidate for three days without success. I had several alternative numbers and was able to make the call. The lesson here is to make sure you can be reached. If you do not have a message phone, provide the name of a relative or friend who will always know how to reach you.

Message phones are a modern aggravation that we seem not to be able to live without. Most people claim they hate to leave messages but will leave them anyway. The content of the message has a lot to do with it. A long message (over 10 or 15 seconds) is a turnoff. Cutesy comments, singing messages, or celebrity impersonations are out. My preference is short and sweet: "Hello, this is Dave Moore. I'm out right now, but if you'll leave your name, phone number, a good time to call back, and any message, I'll get back to you. Thank you." Forget the "Have a nice day" or other trivialities.

If you're on the sending end of a phone message, leave a clear message. I have stopped counting the garbled and incomplete messages I have received. The frustration I feel when I hear something like "This is Bill Jonszzzztizzzz. (21z) 55?-????2 [click]" does not make me feel good about the caller. When I take my messages, I sit with pencil poised, but I can't write down what I don't hear or what goes by me in three seconds. I'm not looking for long messages, but I do prefer for callers to speak slowly ("Hello, this is Bill Johnston. That's spelled J-O-H-N-S-T-O-N"); lead in to what they are saying ("My telephone number is 2 1 3-5 5 5-1 2 3 4"); give me a hint about why they called so I can be prepared ("This is in reference to your job application at the ABC Company"); and give me a time to call back ("I can be reached after 4:00 P.M. on Monday").

A final point on using message phones is to always call back on the messages you receive. If you fail to return calls, the people who might normally leave you a message will simply hang up. They might try to reach you again or they might not. If you don't get a message, you'll never know. Returning phone calls, even messages, is a common courtesy. Why people who would never think of missing a face-to-face appointment think nothing of ignoring a callback request is difficult to understand. Call back on those calls you know are only sales calls. It's a good habit to develop, and it will give you an opportunity to develop effective sales resistance.

Message Services

Message or answering services are similar to message phones except that they provide a real person to interact with instead of a machine. For a modest monthly fee, you switch your phone over to a message service when you are not available. Normally, the services are satisfactory, but sometimes they get overloaded and it takes several rings to reach them; often the caller's patience runs out before the call is answered. You can be sure that they will never tell you, "You had a call but they hung up before we could answer it." If you choose to use a message service, test it by calling yourself and leaving a message at different times. Evaluate it as to the number of rings it takes to answer, courtesy, and the accuracy of the message.

Voice Mail

Voice mail is a system many companies use to receive incoming messages directed to individual employees. It is effective, but some caution should be used. If there is any chance of interception or monitoring of these messages by your current company, you must either caution the caller or direct these calls to another phone. A cardinal principle of the job search is to protect your current job. I call this the "Wing-

Walking Principle," which means that you do not let go of one job until you have a firm hold on the next one.

Car Phone

Car phones are a mixed bag. Like any other communication device, they are useful in a job search. The ability to be reached at any place or any time is convenient, but whether that degree of access is necessary in a job search is questionable. Car phones are expensive, both the equipment and the service. The need to be in contact is a personal decision, but, unless you already have a car phone, I would advise against installing one solely for the purpose of a job search.

If you feel the need to be accessible, a cheaper alternative is a pager or "beeper" service. Many technical professionals (particularly technicians who work in customer environments) already have them and may be able to use them for quicker contacts on a job search.

Telephone Courtesy

In the discussion on message phones, I stressed the importance of returning calls. This is a basic courtesy. Somehow the idea that the same rules of courtesy that apply to other aspects of social interaction do not apply to the telephone has infected our society. I have heard people talk to others in tones and language that they would never use face to face. Perhaps they feel they can get away with such conduct because the other person is unable to attack them physically. Regardless of the reason, discourtesy on the telephone is as unacceptable as any other type of discourtesy.

Courtesy on the telephone is a must for the job seeker. Since the telephone is the job seeker's primary tool, using it in a way that might be detrimental is unwise. How many times have you called a business and been greeted with a curt response or surly tone? How did you feel about it? Whenever I hire a new secretary or receptionist, I call in to my office and pretend to be a stranger. My purpose is to see how this person handles the call.

The magic words "please," "thank you," "may I," and "would you" can work wonders on the telephone. Perhaps we've become sensitized to rude treatment, but nevertheless, a little courtesy will go a long way.

I usually pride myself on my ability to remain courteous in the face of rude treatment, but I did lose my patience on one occasion. I had been trying to reach a company vice president, and his secretary seemed to take great pleasure in keeping her boss free of unscheduled or unwanted calls. Since I had been asked to call and I knew the source of the secretary's efforts was due in large measure to the attitude of her employer, I persisted. I was using all my "power techniques" (see Chapter 6), and she kept insisting that I share my message with her so she could determine whether or not he should be disturbed. My information was of a private nature, and I told her so. Normally, that is enough to get you through, but she persisted. I knew her boss to be a man who shares the same sense of humor that I do, and I sensed that his secretary was overstepping her authority in her efforts to screen his calls. When she said to me "I can't pass a message to Mr. ——————— unless you give me all the details," I replied to her, "Well, this is very confidential, but since you insist on having the information, please tell Mr. ——————— that the little girl's parents have decided not to prosecute!" Later, the boss and I had a laugh over the shock that the secretary went into.

In addition to what you say and how you say it, telephone courtesy includes how you physically handle the phone. Holding the mouthpiece up to your mouth so that what you say is loud and clear, speaking clearly and enunciating your words, and minimizing background noise are all forms of courtesy.

Chapter 6, "Peopleware," will address the interpersonal skills that will make you a "power telephone user."

THE U.S. MAIL

If people ever stopped looking for jobs, the U.S. Postal Service would go out of business. Every day I receive at least ten unsolicited résumés. This is interesting, considering that I no longer advertise. I only list the name of my company in the Yellow Pages, and rely solely on referral business. Companies that advertise for positions or are highly visible receive literally an avalanche of résumés and job inquiries. If job seekers want to know why they seldom hear from employers concerning their résumés, this is the reason. However, it is only one of many.

Although I don't advocate a mail campaign as the best or even an effective way of conducting a job search, it is the method most often used. Since this is the case, people are going to continue to mail résumés and cover letters regardless of what I might say or how ineffective using the mail might be. However, there *are* ways to use the mail that might produce better results. A discussion of these may be beneficial.

Standard Mail Services

Using the mail means more than stuffing an envelope and sticking it into a mailbox. There are several services available and ways to use them to your advantage.

First Class Mail

First class mail is the standard letter. Your correspondence to employers will always go first class. Most first class letters will reach a local (within 50 miles) address in one day and anywhere in the United States within three days.

First class postage is measured by the ounce. A classic mistake made by job hunters is to stuff an envelope with a résumé, cover letter, letters of recommendation, and general personal hype, and then slap a single stamp on the envelope and send it on its way. Sometimes a letter that's slightly overweight will go through, but it is more likely to be delivered with postage due or returned. You should hope that it gets returned. A postage scale is a modest and worthwhile investment that will help you avoid this problem. If there is ever any doubt, put on an extra stamp.

Overnight and Express Mail

There are several private companies in addition to the U. S. Postal Service that offer overnight service. These include Federal Express, DHL, Airborne, and United Parcel Service (UPS), among others. The service is more expensive for parcels of one pound or less, but the extra expense can be worthwhile if you want to get attention.

When an express parcel comes into an office, the assumption is that it must contain something important that requires immediate attention. This ensures that your résumé will get at least a glance, although if a secretary gets it first, it may end up on the heap with all the others. One way to avoid this is to send your package to the hiring authority or manager by name and require a signature as receipt. This will get you attention, but there is a risk that the manager will react negatively. My choice would be to take the risk. You are confident of your background and want to get noticed by the hiring authority. People who claim that they are looking for high-quality employees then resent it when they hear from them are not likely to be good people to work for anyway.

Sending a letter by Express Mail gives you a valid excuse to call to learn whether it arrived. You can do this with first class mail also, but with Express Mail there is a time factor implied and a built-in reason for calling.

Stamps

There are stamps and there are stamps. Direct mail specialists say that commemorative stamps give better results than the common variety and get more attention. They also add a personalized appearance to the envelope. Using commemorative stamps is recommended, but be careful not to imply a negative message with the stamp. A human resources director once commented to me on his reaction to the use of a stamp commemorating American labor as indicating support of unions. Since he spent a large portion of his time contending with unions, this stamp was objectionable to him.

Do not use a postage meter, because this implies that you

are using the assets of your current company for your job search. If you take from your present employer, it can be assumed that you'll probably do the same to a future employer.

Envelopes

Envelopes for correspondence to prospective employers should be white or some neutral shade. They should contain a return address in the upper left hand corner (either printed, typed, or on a label). Never use an envelope from your current company. An envelope is more than just a carrier for what's inside. It tells the recipient who it is from and whether the sender cared enough to spell the recipient's name correctly and get the address right. There is an opportunity for a small expression of professionalism with the envelope, and you should take it seriously.

Envelopes should be business size (No. 10—$9^{1/2}''$ wide). If you are sending a large amount of material that might be too bulky for a standard business envelope, use a large manila envelope (page size—$9'' \times 12''$).

Addresses should be typed or at least neatly printed. Window envelopes are satisfactory and can save typing if you are doing a mass mailing. Window envelopes give a businesslike appearance and indicate that there is something personal inside for the recipient.

Post Office Boxes

Putting a post office box on the return address gives the impression that the sender doesn't want the receiver to know where he or she lives. It also gives the impression that the writer moves often. A job seeker wants to look stable. This means a steady job record and a permanent place of residence.

If your job requires frequent travel or out-of-town work, you can indicate that fact and request that replies be forwarded to your post office box.

FAX MACHINES

The facsimile machine, or "fax," is another technological wonder. We can now "fax" hardcopy in the form of résumés and cover letters directly into the employer's office. The fax also has an aura of importance; anything that comes out of it is likely to receive immediate attention. As these machines proliferate, this sense of urgency will diminish, but for now use it to your advantage.

An effective method is to identify the technical manager who has job openings in your area of expertise. When you make telephone contact, present your background and discuss employment possibilities. The manager is almost sure to ask for a résumé, and when that happens say, "I'll fax it to you immediately. What is your fax number?" If you're on a separate phone, stay on it and fax immediately on the fax line. Ask the employer whether the résumé came across all right and what additional information might be desired. Then say, "I'm available to meet with you Thursday afternoon or Friday morning. Which would be best?"

COMPUTER BULLETIN BOARDS

There are myriad computer bulletin boards, and many of them are in companies that have technical job openings in your field. Many of these list job openings and allow you to leave messages describing your background.

Before contacting a company bulletin board, you should have a concise presentation of your background prepared. By concise I mean less than 100 words. If you attempt to enter your entire résumé or launch into a wordy description, you will lose effectiveness. Use short, terse sentences and key your strengths to the company's job description. Leave your phone number and the hours when you can be reached.

Some commercial data bases (e.g., Prodigy®) also allow you to leave messages indicating that you're looking for a job. I don't know how effective they are, but any opportunity should be exploited.

WORD PROCESSORS

Word processing is the most commonly used personal computer software application. There are more word processing programs sold each year than any other type of software. *Word processing* is the term used for the process that manages and manipulates printed text documents. It replaces all the activities normally performed by a typewriter. There are many advantages of using word processing instead of a typewriter, but the primary one is being able to store documents permanently in the computer or on a disk and call them back for editing. When you type on a computer keyboard, the words appear on the CRT screen and can be manipulated and edited before they are stored as text or recalled later for further editing.

Several years ago, when I was first introduced to word processing, I wondered why I had waited so long. I was a longtime typewriter user and a fair typist. The word processor expanded my typing capability immensely. Although I have a master's degree in computer systems and management information systems, my practical experience with computers was limited to programming. Until my introduction to word processing, I was not a practical user of the computer. I am now a firm believer that no one should graduate from high school or college without the ability to keyboard and use computer productivity tools—especially a word processor.

Why Use a Word Processor?

A word processor gives the user the ability to produce professional-appearing, error-free text. If you've ever read a typewritten page that is full of erasures, strikeovers, and misspellings, you know what a bad impression such a document gives. This is the last impression you would want to leave if that document were your résumé or cover letter. An introduction like that would say that you are careless, sloppy, and incapable of producing a high-quality document.

Please notice that I didn't say that a word processor will keep you from making errors, strikeovers, or any of the problems that your fingers can get into on a keyboard. In fact, as I type this manuscript, I am dancing all over the keyboard, backspacing, typing over, and changing words I don't like. The difference is that I can get away with it because the word processor is structured to handle these activities and still turn out good-looking work.

If you are currently a word processor user, congratulations! If you are not, I urge you become one as soon as possible. Computers are now competitive with office typewriters in price, and they are infinitely more versatile. Even when purchased with a letter-quality printer, the cost at the low end will be around $1,000.

Your primary concern is the quality of output or print. For the best, I recommend a laser printer. There are several personal laser printers on the market that can be purchased for about $1,000. Two in this category are the Hewlitt-Packard HP IIP and the Canon LBP-4®. These produce professional-quality output and are capable of near-typeset quality. They can output graphics and are often used for desktop publishing.

Word Processing Features

Some of the features found on most popular commercial word processors include the following:

- *Insertion and deletion* allows you to insert text into existing text or type over text you don't want.

- *Word wrap and justification* means you don't have to worry about carriage control, and both the left and right margins are justified, or evenly blocked.

- *Page formatting* gives you the ability to change a page, if you don't like the looks of it, by defining margins on the left, right, top, or bottom.

- *Search and replace* gives you the flexibility to find a word or phrase and replace it with another one of your liking without reading the entire document.

- *Block moves and boilerplating* is the ultimate in text preparation; you can move the text around or insert text of your liking without a pair of scissors. The process is called "cut and paste," but it's all done electronically.

- *Character formatting* lets you choose the type and size of font; roman, bold, or italicized type; and underlining.

- Other features include a built-in *spellchecker, thesaurus, stylechecker,* and *page previewer.*

An important term to word processing users is *WYSIWYG.* Pronounced "wizzy-wig," it is an acronym for "What You See Is What You Get." With this feature, the documents and graphics produced on your word processor are displayed on the screen the way they will be printed. You are able to see the different typefaces and features such as boldface and underlining just as they will appear on your printed document. This is a useful feature because on most word processors without the WYSIWYG feature, letters that appear on the screen have the same size and appearance regardless of the font type or size you have selected, which makes the finished product difficult to visualize. Typeface changes and printing features are controlled through "control characters" that appear on the screen. Therefore, you must be concerned with symbols that translate items such as line height (to accommodate different size fonts), underlining, boldface, justification, and margins. The WYSIWYG feature allows you to preview and make changes on your work.

Using a Word Processor on the Job Search

Even if the only reason to use a word processor on a job search were to produce professional-looking résumés, F-A-Bs, and correspondence, I would consider it a very wise use. But, in addition to producing good-looking and error-free documents, word processors allow you the freedom to add variety and individuality to your work. A major problem with résumés is that they are guesses about what a prospective employer might be looking for in a new employee. Word processors permit insertion and deletion of material as well as customization. Each résumé, F-A-B, or letter sent out in support of your job search must be directed at a specific employer. This is particularly critical for technical professions. Skills and definitive qualifications are key issues for technical positions, and the more precisely these can be tied to a job requirement, the greater the likelihood that the employer will want to bring you in for a face-to-face interview.

Overviews of Popular Word Processors

WordPerfect

WordPerfect® is currently the most popular word processing program. It was first introduced in 1980 and is now in release number 5.1. (This means that the product has had five major revisions plus one modification in the last, or fifth, revision.) I would hesitate to say that WordPerfect has become the standard, but it is used in so many offices and is so widespread that its manufacturer could easily make that claim. Because of its popularity, myriad "add-on" software packages have been developed to supplement it. These include dictionaries (even for specialties such as law or medicine), thesauruses, grammar checkers, and presentation graphics programs.

WordPerfect is an excellent choice for a full-featured word processor. It is supported by virtually every printer manufacturer on the market, and most popular software packages (e.g., data base packages such as dBASE III® and dBASE IV® and spreadsheet packages such as Lotus 1-2-3®) will permit export, import, and exchange of data with it.

One feature of interest to the job hunter is WordPerfect's ability to create a mailing list and labels. Another useful feature is its limited desktop publishing capability and the ability to preview documents as they will appear when printed.

A disadvantage of WordPerfect is actually one of its attractions: It is so packed with features that it is overkill for most needs of the average job hunter. If you need a word processor for other uses as well as one that will fulfill your job search needs, however, WordPerfect is an excellent choice.

An important consideration in selecting any software is the support available from its manufacturer. On this count, WordPerfect is first class. An 800 telephone number is available that offers technical support. I have assisted many clients with the installation of WordPerfect, and the support is the best I have encountered from any software company. This is not a casual statement, because the competition among software developers is high and technical support by the leading companies is generally very good. The response is friendly and competent, and it extends to installation of printers and complementary products as well as specific problems with the product.

The question that is probably asked most frequently about software packages is how difficult is it to learn them. On this count, WordPerfect gets high marks. It is reported to be very "user-friendly," or easy to use. It has an excellent "help" system imbedded in it that is just a keystroke away. There are also numerous training programs available including public education at colleges and adult education courses. In addition to extensive training and user manuals provided by the manufacturer, there are supplementary manuals to fit every level of expertise available at commercial bookstores.

WordStar

WordStar® is the Grandaddy of the full-featured word processors, originally introduced in 1978. At the time, it was the competition for the expensive dedicated word processing machines being used commercially. Over the years, it has undergone many changes. In 1984, WordStar 2000 was introduced, and it has built a following over the years.

Over 3 million copies of WordStar have been sold, making it the most widely used software package. Its editing commands have been integrated into many other software packages and notebook systems. For example, the popular dBASE III/IV data base package by Ashton-Tate uses WordStar editing commands.

The current version of WordStar is version 6.0. To give you an idea of the difference between earlier versions and the latest, the current version consists of 28 standard 5.25-inch diskettes while early versions could be fitted on one diskette with space remaining for data. Many of the current diskettes are for printer drivers, large dictionaries and thesauruses, outline programs, and graphics.

WordStar, like WordPerfect, offers a full-featured system that might be more than the average user wants. It does offer a feature called "Advanced page preview," which allows the user to see what the finished document will look like including different fonts and graphics. This valuable feature gives WordStar a limited desktop publishing capability.

WordStar is moderately complex, with many commands to learn. An excellent "help" system with pull-down windows and menus overcomes this somewhat, but it may be intimidating to the neophyte user.

I am a WordStar user and so am probably prejudiced in favor of it. It was my first microcomputer word processing package, and I have watched it develop over the years. I find it no more difficult than WordPerfect, and it serves me well. It offers excellent support, and plenty of add-on software is available.

Examples of word processors and where to get additional information are included at the end of this chapter.

DATA BASE MANAGEMENT SYSTEMS

A *data base* is a collection of data organized into files. A *file* is a collection of *records* containing *fields* that hold data in the form of *characters*. *Data* is the Latin word for "facts." *Information* or the useful product of information or data processing involves the manipulation or processing of data in order to produce useful output. What I've just described is called the *data hierarchy*. It is the structure by which data are logically organized and stored.

A *data base management system*, or *DBMS*, is a software program designed to access, retrieve, and display data from the data base. Before data base management systems were developed, extracting and displaying data was a laborious procedure. It was necessary to write a program for each specific data display. You would have to be a programmer or have access to one, and the process was usually time consuming, expensive, and inconvenient. As a result, information was not readily available except to a few, and certainly not to the average job seeker.

A common misconception is that technical professionals are also computer whizzes. The technical field that encompasses computers is a broad one, and the segment where personal and useful applications are found is only one small part. While many technical fields use computers as tools in support of particular disciplines, it does not mean that the technical professionals in those fields are using computers and, more specifically, personal computers, as personal productivity tools. For example, although I worked as a systems manager and designer, I did not learn how to use a personal computer effectively until several years later.

It is my belief that all professional people, technical and otherwise, should be what is now called *computer literate*. You will find numerous definitions for this term but I believe that in today's society every person who is considered to be a professional or, for that matter, just wants to get ahead, should be reasonably proficient with a word processor, a data base management system, and a spreadsheet. Fortunately, more and more people are realizing the benefits of the PC.

Using a DBMS in the Job Search

A DBMS is a method for storing, retrieving, and displaying information. While the context in which we are discussing it is computer based, it can be manual. In fact, most data base management systems are manual, for example, telephone books, catalogs, address lists, personal files, and so forth. The computer should be viewed as a tool to simplify and automate the process of organizing and using a DBMS.

The job seeker can simplify the search process by storing information on potential employers, their addresses, telephone numbers, contact information, correspondence dates, interview dates, follow-up contacts, feedback, outcomes, and a variety of other useful information. For a short job search involving only a few employers, a manual system might do the job. However, if the job search is extensive and continues over a period of several months, a manual system will quickly become large and unwieldly. Electronic manipulation of data is much faster and more versatile than any manual system.

Drawbacks to Using a DBMS

Even popular DBMS packages such as dBASE III or IV, R:BASE,® Paradox,® or Q&A™ have drawbacks. First, they are relatively expensive. Ashton-Tates' dBASE III and IV will sell at discount prices for around $300 to $400. There are cheaper systems for $100 or less, and they should be evaluated for suitability. The best way to check for suitability is to talk with system users and compare their uses with your planned uses. Second, while they are relatively easy to use, there is learning required. This must be measured against the urgency of your job search and the utility you expect to achieve. Third, some of them—for example, dBASE III and IV—use programming to some extent for a few applications. If your use will require programming, you should again consider the value expected versus the cost in time you will have to devote. Finally, you should consider whether you have uses beyond your job search. A one-shot use will not justify a large expenditure of money and time, and perhaps you should use something that will do a satisfactory job but is more user friendly and cheaper.

Examples of data base management systems are included at the end of this chapter.

INFORMATION AND CONTACT TRACKING SYSTEMS

Contact tracking systems are a form of DBMS that were developed as simple-to-use systems to enable salespeople and their managers to keep track of clients and prospects. You may encounter these systems under the generic names of "client management" or "prospecting" systems.

Most of these systems were originally developed with sales and marketing in mind. Instead of providing a package from which you can design and develop a DBMS of your choosing, contact tracking systems are designed with predefined fields that reflect operations in a sales environment. If predefined reports are included, they reflect sales and sales representative activities. Most later versions have added a report generator to enable users to create reports designed for their own requirements rather than merely reflecting what the system designer thought might be needed.

The feature that is of greatest value—particularly to the job seeker—is a built-in word processor or a user-friendly interface to a commercial word processor. This feature is usually limited to creating letters and simple documents.

The advantage of contact tracking systems is their simplicity and ease of use. They are excellent for maintaining names and addresses of prospective employers and the activities that have been accomplished with them (e.g., résumés sent, interview, follow-up calls, or job offers). Their word processing features are usually oriented to letter writing and address merging, which is the most useful feature of a word processor or DBMS for the job search. This combination of word processing and DBMS with a built-in interface greatly simplifies these functions for the job seeker.

The disadvantage of these software packages is that they have built-in limitations. They were designed to be applied to specific uses, and they do not include the option of custom design for other applications the user may have.

I have used a contact tracking system called The Selling System™ for several years, and even though I am also a user of the dBASE DBMS and the WordStar word processor, I use The Selling System exclusively when addressing and mailing correspondence.

Examples of client management/contact tracking systems are included at the end of this chapter.

PERSONAL INFORMATION MANAGEMENT SYSTEMS

Personal information management systems (PIMs) are also called *desktop managers* because they are designed to perform a variety of functions that support personal or desktop organization. These functions include address maintenance (automated "rotary address files"), text search and retrieval, data file creation, calendar and appointment maintenance, and low-level word processing.

I recently began using a PIM called Arriba,™ and of all the different software applications available for job search support, my personal choice would be a personal information manager. It is easy to use and embodies all the desirable features of word processors, data base management systems, and contact trackers/client managers. Its simplicity makes it an excellent choice for someone who does not want to invest a great deal of time in learning a complex system.

In order to describe the functions of a PIM, I will describe Arriba and use it as a representative system. There are several others on the market, and my recommendation would be to select one that fills your personal needs and preferences. The most elegant (an expensive) is Lotus Agenda.® It claims to use artificial intelligence/expert system routines, but it is also more complex and difficult to learn and use.

Arriba

Arriba collects and organizes information in "folders" and "notes." This permits you to enter information free form and place it into "folders" just as you would if you were filing information manually. When you retrieve a folder, it displays a list of the "notes" contained in it. You can also cross reference notes from one folder to another. An Arriba screen showing the display of "folders" and "notes" is shown in Figure 5–1.

Arriba uses a full text search technique to locate information. Unlike a DBMS, you don't have to use a predefined key word to retrieve information. If you can remember any part of the note, all information pertaining to that reference will be compiled into an electronic folder and displayed. This includes all address lists, data base files, and correspondence contained in the system. An example of the text search feature is shown in Figure 5–2.

A telephone list is available that can track companies, addresses, phone numbers, and individual contacts (see Figure 5–3). This list can be organized by category (e.g.,

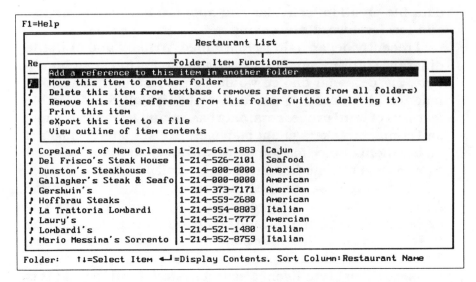

FIGURE 5–1. Arriba collects and organizes information in *Folders* and *Notes.* When you open a *Folder,* Arriba displays a list of what's inside—including *Notes* and other *Folders.* Arriba can create columns to view and sort key pieces of information. It also cross references *Notes* from one *Folder* to another and wherever text is attached to a *Note,* Arriba marks the addition with a musical note symbol. *Reprinted by permission of Good Software Corporation.*

hiring authorities) and then output to envelopes, labels, and letters.

Arriba also allows you to create data base files containing up to 25 fields per record. This feature is used when you need a more structured format. Information contained in a record can be expanded by attaching a "note" in a more free and unstructured format. A sample record is shown in Figure 5–4.

A feature that is a must for job hunters is *Arriba's* calendar. You can schedule interviews, calls, follow-up activities, and letters and cross-reference them with the *notes* and *folders* features. This is important, because your activity level will increase during a job search and you can't afford to miss calls or appointments. It is also necessary that you keep up with the demands of your current job and schedule. The calendar screen is shown in Figure 5–5.

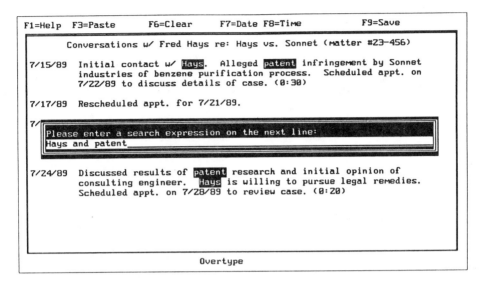

```
F1=Help  F3=Paste      F6=Clear     F7=Date F8=Time        F9=Save

        Conversations w/ Fred Hays re: Hays vs. Sonnet (matter #Z3-456)

 7/15/89  Initial contact w/ Hays.  Alleged patent infringement by Sonnet
          industries of benzene purification process.  Scheduled appt. on
          7/22/89 to discuss details of case. (0:30)

 7/17/89  Rescheduled appt. for 7/21/89.

 7/
        Please enter a search expression on the next line:
        Hays and patent

 7/24/89  Discussed results of patent research and initial opinion of
          consulting engineer.  Hays is willing to pursue legal remedies.
          Scheduled appt. on 7/28/89 to review case. (0:20)




                              Overtype
```

FIGURE 5–2. Arriba has a *Full-Text Search Feature* which locates any piece of information in seconds. This extends to any string of characters in the *Note* not just key words as in most Data Base Management Systems. Arriba will seek out everything in the system that refers to that information and cross reference it into a new *Folder. Reprinted by permission of Good Software Corporation.*

The PIM is the best overall application I have found yet for tracking and supporting a job search. I recommended *Arriba* to a friend, and he calls me weekly to rave about it. It's a versatile system, and he has found a variety of uses for it.

A list of PIMs is included at the end of the chapter.

RÉSUMÉ-WRITING SYSTEMS

Résumé-writing systems are tools designed specifically for the job search. These are low-level word processors preformatted with templates of various types of résumés. Although the primary function of these tools is to assist in the preparation of your résumé, each contains other features that should be evaluated for usefulness and applicability to your needs. These features include WYSIWYG page previewing, word

```
F1=Help

                        Main Phone List
  ┌──────────────────┬──────────────────────────────────┬────────────────────┐
  │ Last Name        │ First┌Phone List Print Functions─┐│ Company/Reference  │
  ├──────────────────┼──────│ List of titles            ││────────────────────│
  │ Baumann          │ Tamar│ Mailing list              ││ Index Corp.        │
  │ Black            │ Leann│ Contents of address note  ││ Black Enterprises  │
  │ Bolt             │ Garon│ Envelopes                 ││ Boltonics,Inc      │
  │ Bounds           │ Byron│ comma-Delimited list      ││ G.T.I.             │
  │ Brown            │ Jeffr└───────────────────────────┘│ Classic Cars       │
  │ Carlson, M.D.    │ Eric              (214) 520-8967  │ Doctor             │
  │ Chappel          │ Cynthia           (201) 345-7688  │ Blue Max Interprises│
  │ Clausell         │ Mary              (214) 363-2721  │ Alloy Products, Inc.│
  │ Crenshaw         │ William           (412) 357-0916  │ Park Corporation   │
  │ Durban           │ Bill              (214) 412-0094  │ Struthers Company  │
  │ Faction          │ Diane             (817) 660-7612  │ Lineman Corporation│
  │ Foul             │ Lisa              (214) 341-1869  │ BAC Industries     │
  │ Fritch           │ Anna              (818) 651-0111  │ Advantage Sales Corp.│
  │ Garrison         │ Jason             (214) 250-0098  │ Friend             │
  │ Gelfling         │ Aaron             (214) 484-7581  │ Science Research   │
  │ Griffith         │ Debra             (817) 660-7612  │ Lineman Corporation│
  │ Halek            │ Terri             (512) 241-8990  │ G.T.I.             │
  └──────────────────┴───────────────────────────────────┴────────────────────┘
  Folder:   ↑↓=Select Item  ⏎=Display Contents. Sort Column:Last Name
```

FIGURE 5–3. A single keystroke opens Arriba's *Phone List*. The first few letters of a name is all that is required to open the Phone List at that entry. There is the capability of creating multiple lists then organizing them by category and printing envelopes and mailing labels. There is also an autodial capability which permits dialing numbers that appear on the screen. Also, each person on the Phone List has a personal *Folder* where *Notes* can be kept on phone conversations, memos, and related information. *Reprinted by permission of Good Software Corporation.*

processing (low level), sample letters, contact tracking data bases, appointment-scheduling calendars, career advice, and interviewing-skills tutorials. Not all of these features are found in all systems that claim to be résumé-writing systems, so you should evaluate each package according to your specific desires.

Résumé-writing systems are useful, but they are relatively unsophisticated. This is reflected in the price of the various packages, which is under $50. The primary use for these products is résumé formatting, and they are easy to use. If you require a wider variety of features and they are not included in the résumé-writing system you are considering, some of the other software packages discussed here might be

```
F1=Help    F3=Paste    F6=Clear    F7=Date    F8=Time    F9=Save
                         Commercial Listings
                      ═Real Estate Form═
Property Name: [            ]
Contact:       [            ]          Phone: [            ]
Address:       [            ]
City:          [            ]    St: [  ]   Zip: [    ]

Area of City:  [          ]      Map Coordinate: [        ]
Year Built:    [    ]

Asking Price: $[        ]         Occupancy: [  ]%
Price/Sq Ft: $[ .00]  Rent/Sq Ft: $[ .00]      Expenses/Sq Ft: $[ .00]
Total Sq Ft: [      ]  Rentable Sq Ft: [       ]  Usable Sq Ft: [       ]

Comments: [                    ]


                          Overtype
```

FIGURE 5–4. Arriba permits creation of *Custom Forms* for tracking up to 25 pieces of information. This useful data base feature is enhanced through the cross-referencing of attached *Notes. Reprinted by permission of Good Software Corporation.*

a better choice. Representative résumé-writing systems are listed at the end of this chapter.

SELECTION AND USE OF COMPUTER SOFTWARE

Several types of software that can be used to support a job search have been discussed. Within each type are specific packages. Selecting the type of software that would best suit your needs, then choosing among the many packages available is not an easy task.

Software selection should be approached from a pragmatic point of view. A classic error that is made when selecting software is to choose the package and then consider how it will be used. The worst criterion used is price. Buying a computer or a software package because it is cheap is the worst mistake that can be made. Software must be chosen on

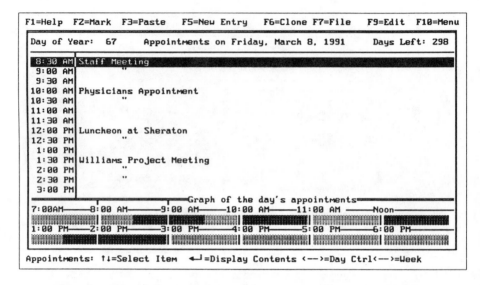

FIGURE 5–5. Appointments and schedules are maintained in Arriba's *Built-In Calendar,* which displays times for meetings on its appointment pages. Additional information concerning any appointment can be attached with a *Note. Reprinted by permission of Good Software Corporation.*

the basis of utility. Cheap software that is not used or fails to perform as expected is not a bargain.

Make a list of the tasks you want to accomplish during your job search. Then look at the various software packages and compare their capabilities. When you find suitable software candidates, ask around to find people who have used them and seek their comments and recommendations. When you have narrowed your choices down to two or three packages, select the one you like best. At that point, the differences are probably slight, so it's safe to go with your personal preference.

Software can be useful to your job search. It should never be viewed as a substitute for hard work, but as a labor- and time-saving supplement.

SUMMARY

Modern technology has provided the job seeker with a variety of tools that can be used to great advantage in the job search.

Among these are the telephone, which encompasses facsimile or "fax" services, call waiting and automatic answering features, voice mail, and paging. The technology that has brought the greatest support to job seekers is the personal computer (PC).

The PC's most significant contribution is the economical word processor, which offers to the job hunter affordable typing and document preparation including automated résumé-writing systems. Data base management systems, information and contact tracking systems, and personal information managers are forms of data manipulation and handling software that permit the job hunter to organize, track, and manage a long and complex job search.

Hardware and software should always be considered as support tools for your job hunting efforts, not as the means to reach your career goals. Use them in that manner and they will serve you well.

Representative Software Suitable for the Job Search

The following software packages are representative of the various types of applications that are available to support job search activities:

WORD PROCESSING

WordPerfect®

WordPerfect Corporation
1555 N. Technology Way
Orem, UT 84057
(801) 222-4050

WordPerfect word processing software is available for IBM Personal Computers and compatibles and the Apple MacIntosh. In addition to full-featured word processing, WordPerfect offers a compatible spreadsheet package, a menu-driven database package, a calendar, and an information management system. Also available are networking and international versions of the software.

WordStar®

WordStar International
201 Alameda del Prado
Novato, CA 94949
(415) 382-8000

WordStar offers 14 different language versions (including a multilingual thesaurus) in release 6.0. It features support for a variety of laser and conventional printers including the Hewlett-Packard LaserJet III and the Canon LBP-8 Mark III. It is available for IBM Personal Computers and compatibles.

DATA BASE MANAGEMENT SYSTEMS

dBASE IV®

Ashton-Tate Corporation
20101 Hamilton Avenue
Torrance, CA 90502
(213) 329-8000

dBASE is the oldest and the most popular of the various DBMS packages now on the market. Its current version is dBASE IV, release 1.1. dBASE offers its own programming language and permits import and export of its data files for mailmerge to most popular word processing packages. In spite of its popularity and widespread use, dBASE is considered to be more difficult to learn and use than some of the DBMS software developed more recently. On the plus side, there is a wide variety of training courses and facilities available, in addition to a broad familiarity with it among the programming community.

R:BASE®

Microrim, Inc.
3925 159th Ave., N.E.
Redmond, WA 98052
(206) 649-9500

R:BASE is touted as an extremely user friendly and easy to use relational DBMS. It uses a function called "Application Express," which allows users and programmers the ability to create applications without programming. It has a fourth generation language for programming (easy-to-use, English-like expressions) and directly reads and writes dBASE files.

Paradox®

Borland International, Inc.
1800 Green Hills Road
Scotts Valley, CA 95067
(408) 438-8400

Paradox is a relational DBMS that is becoming increasingly popular. It is considered to be easy to use. Its manufacturer, Borland International, is known for topnotch, high-quality software. Its award winning Sidekick® desktop management system and Quattro Pro® spreadsheet software are considered by many experts to be the best in their category. With the excellent support offered by Borland, Paradox is a fine choice for any data base requirements.

CONTACT TRACKING SYSTEMS

The Selling System™   *Pyramid Software Inc.*
                                    21035 Calle Matoral
                                    El Toro, CA 92630
                                    (714) 859-0468

The Selling System has been used by the author for over six years. Used to track employer clients, it maintains extensive contact history and appointment information. Combined with an excellent letter writing feature that supports label making and data base management, it is an easily learned system that was originally developed for salespeople who required organization and management of client contacts. It also features a report generator and excellent data import and export characteristics.

Totall Manager®   *Bartel Software*
             948 East 7145 South, Suite C-101
                          Midvale, UT 84047
                           (800) 777-6368

This program is designed specifically for sales and lead tracking and telemarketing. It maintains comprehensive data bases (up to 94 fields) on prospective clients including detailed contract histories, client profiles, and account status. It also has "to-do" lists, appointment calendars, and user-definable fields. It boasts a word processor, personal expense accounting, and a custom report generator.

PERSONAL INFORMATION SYSTEMS

Arriba™   *Good Software Corporation*
                                13601 Preston Road
                                Dallas, TX 75240
                                (800) 272-GOOD

Versatile and easy to use, Arriba offers the functions of mail list management, letter writing, and data base/text search at a modest cost. It is an excellent organizer and will provide valuable services for the job hunter.

Agenda®

Lotus Development Corporation
55 Cambridge Parkway
Cambridge, MA 02142
(617) 577-8500

Agenda is the PIM offered by Lotus Development, which is the developer of Lotus 1-2-3, the leading spreadsheet application. It is considered to be more difficult to learn than other PIMs, but it offers artificial intelligence and interface with Lotus products. It is a high-quality product but is more expensive than other PIMs on the market.

OnTime®

Campbell Services Inc.
21700 Northwestern Highway, Suite 1070
Southfield, MI 48075
(313) 559-5955

OnTime is a calendar and to-do list manager. It provides keyword search capabilities, single entry of recurring events, automatic rollover of noncompleted "to-do's," and ease of learning and use. It is primarily an appointment system and lacks some of the features of other PIMs. Its price ($69.95 retail) makes it attractive for someone who only wants the features that it offers.

It's About Time™

Pyramid Software Inc.
21035 Calle Matoral
El Toro, CA 92630
(714) 859-0468

It's About Time is a desktop management and calendar/appointment version of Pyramid's contact tracking system, "The Selling System." It has a built-in word processor called "Letter Writer," which has a powerful mailmerge and word processing interface. It provides contact tracking through its appointment function but does not have the data base attributes. An excellent choice, with easy-to-use features.

RÉSUMÉ-WRITING SYSTEMS

RésuméMaker™   *Individual Software, Inc.*
                                        125 Shoreway Road, Suite 3000
                                            San Carlos, CA 94070
                                              (800) 331-3313 or
                                            (800) 822-3522 (CA)

In addition to résumé-preparation guidance, RésuméMaker provides an activities journal, a letter-writing system with helps and guidance (including sample letters), and an appointment scheduler. It also has facilities for creating a data base to track potential employer companies. The retail price is $49.95.

The Perfect Résumé Computer Kit®   *Permax Systems Inc.*
                                             5008 Gordon Avenue
                                            Madison, WI 53716
                                              (608) 222-8804

This system comes in two modules. The first is called "Career Consultant" and is a tutorial discussing subjects such as interests, personal accomplishments, skills, and talents, which assists the job hunter in developing a résumé. The second module is called "Résumé Builder," which provides three résumé formats to assist the job hunter in creating a résumé. The single-user version of The Perfect Résumé Computer Kit is priced at $49.95.

6

THE TOOLS
OF THE TRADE:
"PEOPLEWARE"

Technical job seekers are special because of the special skills and knowledge they possess. They study to learn and apply themselves in order to advance and improve their technical skills. Their talents are what makes them in demand.

While skills and talents may be what employers value, they are not the primary ingredients of what opens doors or gets the job. We have all known people who hold jobs but exhibit a minimum of skills. We shake our heads and wonder how they got such great jobs. These same people also seem to thrive on the job and get promotions while more skilled people fall by the wayside. When they decide to seek new opportunities, they usually find positions as good as or better than their last.

How do these people keep on getting jobs for which they are obviously not qualified? How do they keep them and even move on to something better? The answer is that they possess skills that are independent of technical abilities. These are what are known as "people" or interpersonal skills.

WHAT ARE "PEOPLE" SKILLS?

If asked to define "people" skills in one word, that word would be *communication*. Communication is what enables us to get our points across to others. It's what makes successful salespeople successful, and it's what enables successful job hunters to get the best jobs possible. Effective communication is a vital skill that touches every facet of our lives. Good communicators are usually successful in their personal lives as well as on the job. Unfortunately, communication is a skill that is developed over a long period of time. Fortunately, it's a skill that can be learned and its principles applied immediately.

Most people believe they communicate well. If told there is an art to using something as simple as the telephone effectively, they will respond with "I've been using the telephone all my life. I've never had any problem with it, and there's nothing I can learn." Yes, most people have used the telephone all their lives. Yes, all of us have communicated one way or another all our lives. However, to believe that there is nothing more to learn or no improvement to be made is an unfortunate block to improvement of communications skills.

The purpose of this chapter is to lay a foundation of communication fundamentals. Two specific communications topics—interviewing and personal image—are covered in detail in Chapters 8 and 9.

FUNDAMENTALS OF COMMUNICATION

A Definition

A good approach to understanding communication is to establish a meaning or definition. The *Oxford English Dictionary* refers to the meaning of the word *communication* by going back to its Latin root, *communicare,* which is translated "to make common to many" or to "share." This means that when we communicate we share ideas, feelings, and facts in a manner that is common to those with whom we are sharing them. "Common" in this context means "understanding." A reasonable definition of communication would be "the act or process of sharing facts, ideas, or feelings with others in ways that are understandable to all." Boiling it down even further and making it personal, "Communication is making yourself understood."

Why Misunderstandings Occur

If you have ever played the game of "Telephone" at a party, you have an insight into the dynamics of miscommunication. In the game, the players are seated in a circle and the first player whispers a brief message to the next player, who in turn whispers it to the next, and so on, until the message is passed to the last player. This player then announces the message to the group. The first player then reads the original message and establishes the game's purpose, which is to reveal the humorous differences and distortions that occur between the first and last renderings.

The reason "Telephone" works its confusion is because of the differing frames of reference from which people communicate. A message passed from person to person or up or down an organizational chain of command undergoes changes in the process. These changes include the following:

- *Leveling.* Details get lost or left out.

- *Condensing.* The message gets simplified and shortened.

- *Sharpening.* Details get emphasized and become more important in the message.

- *Assimilating.* Imprecise details are clarified and reinterpreted to conform to the message sender's frame of reference.

- *Embellishing.* Details are added to enhance the message.[1]

The following is a somewhat graphic and tongue-in-cheek example of a message that changed as it was passed along. It came across my fax from an anonymous sender.

In the beginning was the plan
And then came the assumptions
And the assumptions were without form
And the plan was completely without substance
And the darkness was upon the face of the Employees
And they spoke amongst themselves, saying
"It is a crock of shit and it stinks"
And the Employees went unto their Supervisors, saying
"It is a pail of dung and none may abide the odor thereof"
And the Supervisors went unto their Managers, saying
"It is a vessel of fertilizer and none may abide its strength"
And the Directors went unto their Executive Directors, saying
"It contains that which aids plant growth and it is very strong"
And the Executive Directors went unto the General Manager,
saying,
"This new plan will actively promote the growth and
efficiency of this organization and these areas in particular"
And the Board of Directors looked upon the plan and saw
that it was good and the plan became policy.
This is how shit happens!

-Anonymous-

The Symbols and Codes of Communication

Interpersonal communication goes beyond the spoken word. There are three basic communication codes or symbols that we use.

---

[1] Cheryl Hamilton with Cordell Parker, *Communicating for Results* (Belmont, Calif.: Wadsworth, 1990), pp. 12–13.

1. *Language.* This is comprised of spoken or written words that are used to convey ideas and feelings.

2. *Nonverbal signals.* Also called *body language.* These are ways we communicate without words. They include eye contact (or lack of it), facial expressions, gestures, body movement, posture, appearance, or conduct.

3. *Paralanguage.* Before we learned to talk (using language as an individual or as a race), we communicated verbally through grunts, cries, and various other noises and effects. We continue to communicate in this manner at times, but for the most part we now communicate through the structure of language.

Most people, if asked how most interpersonal communication occurs, would likely answer "through the spoken word or language." However, researchers have found that in the average message, only 7 percent of meaning is conveyed through words (language), while 38 percent is by means of associated voice sounds and characteristics (paralanguage) and 55 percent is by body language (nonverbal).[2]

The simple greeting "Good morning, how are you?" can be delivered with a smile or a frown and an angry or happy tone and convey an infinite number of messages. Body language and voice tone and style are often unconscious reflections of our moods and feelings, and too often we send out unintentional meanings. An awareness of not only what we say, but also how we say it and how we act when we say it will go a long way toward improving our communication style.

THE IMPORTANCE OF LANGUAGE

This does not imply that language is not important and that we should confine our communications to nonverbal gestures or body language. The words we use form the founda-

---

[2]Albert Mehrabian, *Silent Messages* (Belmont, Calif.: Wadsworth, 1981), pp. 75–80.

tion of our communication process. Words convey meanings, and our choice of words can make a difference between being understood and being misunderstood.

How often have you encountered brilliant and successful individuals who had difficulty expressing themselves? The fact that they have succeeded in their professional fields is a testimonial to their ability and perhaps greatness, but their limitations in oral communication skills have subtracted from their image. It should be stated that language skills will not ensure success, nor will a lack of language skills necessarily keep a person from succeeding. We all have seen too many examples to the contrary. However, these are exceptions, and language skills give an edge that is well worth having.

As the foundation on which we build our communication skills, language should receive special attention. It is sometimes taken for granted, since it is acquired in early childhood and used continuously. However, language must be nurtured and polished in order to improve it. We must also weed out bad habits that we pick up along the way. Overuse of slang, incorrect grammar, profanity, regional or ethnic accents, and nonverbal noises ("uhs," "ahs," and "you knows," for example) are a few stumbling blocks that get in the way of good language usage.

HOW TO BUILD GOOD LANGUAGE SKILLS

1. *Listen to yourself.* This doesn't mean you should record your words (although it's not a bad idea), but you should be alert to what you say and how you say it. I'm originally from Indiana, and I grew up saying "goin'," comin'," and "swimmin'." The "g" wasn't big enough to fit on my "i-n-g's." I also went to the "crick" instead of the "creek" and a few other regional verbal locations. Overcoming these long-established habits was not easy; it first took an awareness of what I was saying and then a concentrated effort to pronounce the words correctly. Being from the Midwest, my regional accent was less pronounced than that of someone from the Northeast or Deep South. (They might have another opinion!)

Too often people with regional accents wear them like a badge of honor. Being proud of your heritage is admirable until it gets in the way of your getting a job or advancing your career. Then it's time to do something about it. Listen to how you talk. Your goal is to "neutralize" your language—that is, refine it so that it is without recognizable accents or colloquialisms.

If you're from a foreign country and English is a second language, you may have to make a greater effort, but I assure you that it is worth it. It may require that you take diction lessons or enroll in a class for English as a Second Language (ESL). Several years ago, a man from Italy contacted me for help in a job search. He had been in the United States less than a year, and his English was terrible. He spoke a pidgin form of English and scoffed at my suggestions that he enroll in a class to improve his English. He was technically well qualified, and if his language skills had been equal to those of a native English speaker he would have been in great demand. I sent him on 25 interviews before he was hired. The employer was a second-generation Italian-American who spoke Italian fluently and was willing to overlook the English deficiency in favor of the man's technical abilities. I should add that the primary objection of the other employers was the applicant's inability to speak English satisfactorily. Unfortunately, most job seekers won't have the luxury of a prolonged job search to find someone who "talks like they do."

2. *Read.* People who read extensively have larger and better vocabularies and more general knowledge than those who do not read. This goes beyond improved language skills, but knowledge—even trivial knowledge—beyond a technical education and experience will not hurt and could conceivably be helpful. The type of reading depends on your preference, but general fiction and nonfiction not associated with your technical specialization would be my recommendation. This type of reading broadens your perspective and is also recreational and relaxing.

3. *Do crossword puzzles.* For relaxation while expanding your vocabulary and building word skills, crossword puzzles have no equal. A few years ago, I was a contestant on a TV game show. These shows are taped in batches; that is, two weeks' worth of daily shows are taped by doing five shows per day for two consecutive days. In order to get a sufficient number of contestants, they call in more than they need and put them together in a holding room prior to going on the show. There were about 20 contestants, and they did a variety of activities to pass the time. Some read, others conversed with each other, while three worked on crossword puzzles. I don't remember how each fared on the show, but I do remember that all of the crossword puzzle workers were winners. There may not be a direct connection, but these people did well with general knowledge questions. I have since taken up doing crossword puzzles—not with the zeal of the game show contestants I observed, but on a relaxed, spare-time level— and I will attest that it is excellent mental exercise and a great vocabulary builder.

4. *Join Toastmasters International.*® I have attended communication seminars and classes, but I have not found any to equal the value of Toastmasters. The following is the mission of Toastmasters International as stated in its *Communication and Leadership Program Manual:*

> Toastmasters International is the leading movement devoted to making effective oral communication a worldwide reality.
>
> Through its member clubs, Toastmasters International helps men and women learn the arts of speaking, listening and thinking—vital skills that promote self-actualization, enhance leadership potential, foster human understanding, and contribute to the betterment of mankind.
>
> It is basic to this mission that Toastmasters International continually expand its worldwide network of clubs, thereby offering ever-greater numbers of people the opportunity to benefit from its programs.

Joining Toastmasters International is an excellent way to build communication skills. It is not a one-day or one-course effort, but a continuing skill-building program. You will be trained in speaking and listening skills, receive positive correction and critique for your presentations, and have unlimited opportunities to interact, lead, and develop your presentation skills. The cost is modest, and there are thousands of clubs worldwide and in virtually every community in the United States. Many clubs advertise their meeting times and places in local newspapers. For further information about meeting places, the organization, or its program, contact Toastmasters International, Inc., 23182 Arroyo Vista, Rancho Santa Margarita, CA 92688.

BUILDING NONVERBAL (BODY LANGUAGE) SKILLS

Body language is often "spoken" without our knowledge and transmits a message that our spoken words did not say. If this sounds a bit bizarre, consider the following.

You enter the office of the director of research for a job interview. The director is sitting at his desk and does not get up. He says, "Please come in and have a seat, I'll be right with you." You sit down in a chair across from his desk, and, for about one minute, the director finishes reading a document of some sort. He then looks up, folds his arms across his chest, leans back in his chair, and says, "Thank you for coming in, we've been looking for a development engineer for some time, please tell me about yourself." As you start to talk, the director's eyes shift momentarily to a wall clock, then to the paper he was reading, then back to you. You continue speaking. When you have finished a brief overview of your background, the director says, "We've got a new position for an engineer in our department and we're anxious to get started on the project." As he speaks, he twists a paper clip into scrap metal then picks up a pencil and proceeds to doodle on a piece of paper in front of him. As the conversation progresses, you notice he writes something among the doodles. Finally, the director stands up and says, "Well, Mr. _____, thank you for coming in, we'll be getting back to you."

If only the language and words were extracted from this exchange, it could be called a fairly average interview. Since the candidate seemed to be qualified and there were no negative verbal indications on the part of the prospective em-

ployer, there might even be reason to call the interview positive or hopeful. However, there was far more said than came
across in spoken words. The director remained seated when
you entered the room. This could be interpreted as being
rude or busy, and you likely gave him the benefit of the doubt
and called it busy. Because he finished reading something
before starting the interview, you assumed he was busy. As
he leaned back in his chair and folded his arms, you sensed
that something was not right. He should have been interested
in a development engineer: By his own admission he had
been "looking for some time!" He then looked at the clock
and back to the paper he was first reading—possibly he had
an upcoming appointment or perhaps a deadline involving
the paper. The doodling and twisting of the paper clip indicates worry about something.

The nonverbal messages told you that the director's mind
was not on the interview, and therefore it was not the priority
that his words indicated. Whatever his reasons, the director
was telling you nonverbally that you weren't as important as
his other concerns.

Now let's consider the nonverbal messages you sent to
the employer. You probably don't remember, but you very
likely reacted to the director's signals. Much body language
is subconscious; that is, we aren't aware we're doing it. You
may have frowned, raised an eyebrow, or wrinkled your fore-
head—all generally accepted signals of concern, wonder, or
disapproval. You may have shifted in your chair to indicate
concern that your message wasn't getting across and perhaps you leaned into the conversation a bit. Perhaps when
the director looked back to the paper you registered a look of
disgust over his inattention to you.

These signals between you and the interviewer will probably never be mentioned. Only the words will be considered,
and they seemed positive.

INTERPRETING NONVERBAL SIGNALS

Body language can be categorized into conscious and subconscious signals. Conscious signals are those we inten-

tionally send. For example, a wink, a thumbs up, or wave of the hand. Unconscious signals are usually given without our even being aware of them. Unconscious signals also nearly always express our true feelings, regardless of what we are expressing verbally.

Body language is not one gesture or movement. Just as it takes more than one word to form a verbal concept, nonverbal messages are a series of signals and body movements. They must be considered in the context of the situation and the surroundings in which they occur. For example, an upraised hand waved by a student in a classroom has a much different meaning than the same gesture by an individual seeing an acquaintance from across a street.

Body Parts and Their Meanings

The Eyes

There is no other part of the human body to which so much meaning is attached. Sayings such as "An honest man always looks you in the eye" or "The eyes are the windows of the soul" give a hint of how society reads meaning from eyes.

Eye expressions are fairly easy to interpret. *Eye contact* is what is generally interpreted as "looking you in the eye." People tend to break eye contact when an uncomfortable subject is brought up. If the person doing the interviewing tends to look away when you mention a particular topic, shift to another topic and see whether the eye contact is reestablished. Studies have also shown that people rate speakers whose eye contact is greater as being more sincere than those who have less eye contact.[3]

There are some eye gestures and overt movements that have common interpretations in our society. For example, the wink is usually interpreted to mean agreement or a sexual flirtation, depending on the gender of the other party and the circumstances. Raised eyebrows express wonderment or

---

[3] Philip L. Hunsaker and Anthony J. Alessandra, *The Art of Managing People* (Englewood Cliffs, N.J.: Prentice-Hall, 1980), p. 167.

doubt; narrowed eyelids indicate displeasure or anger; and a wide-eyed look projects surprise.

The ability to interpret eye gestures and other body-language signals can be developed and enhanced. Being aware of body language and looking for it in others and yourself will increase your perceptiveness. Associating a gesture or movement with the reaction to it will enable you to improve your ability to utilize this communication skill.

The Head and Face

Head movements and facial expressions are giveaways to feelings and emotions. Nodding or shaking the head normally signals agreement or disagreement, while holding the head downward means embarrassment or hurt and holding the head up means pride. Facial expressions such as a smile, a grimace, gritted teeth, or the mouth held open project nonverbal meanings that have been clearly defined in our society as happiness, disappointment, anger, and surprise, respectively.

The Body

How we hold our body tells others a lot about us, and how others hold their bodies gives us a great deal of information also. As an experiment, observe people walking down the street. Can you spot the ones who are happy? Unhappy? Successful? Failures? You don't know for sure, but the closer they are to one end or the other of an emotional spectrum, the more accurate you will be. As you fine tune your ability to read body language, you will be able to discern more subtle differences.

In an interview or one-on-one conversation, the body language is directed more at you and therefore is easier to understand once you know what signals to look for. If an interviewer begins to lean back in his chair, boredom is beginning to set in and you should understand that the interview is not going well. If an interviewer begins to lean forward and her whole body moves toward you, she is showing greater interest in you and what you have to say. Twisting, fidgeting, and changing positions frequently are classic signs of boredom and/or nervousness.

The Hands and Arms

What people do with their hands and where they put them are indicators of emotions and signals of nonverbal communication. Rubbing the hands together or wringing them normally means the person is nervous and probably stressed. Such people are more difficult to communicate with because they are concerned with other matters and you are not their priority. They are also more likely to disagree with you. Putting the fingers together and forming a "church steeple" projects a type of confidence that signifies a feeling of superiority. If an interviewer is standing and places his hands behind his back and locks them together, you are getting a signal of authority and control. This person views himself as being in charge.

These signals would appear to imply negative communications. However, don't interpret one signal as the entire message. Body language is only a part of the communication process, and it must be viewed in the context of the sender's words and other actions. For example, pulling or rubbing the ear is usually interpreted to mean that the person doesn't understand your message or doubts it. However, it could also mean an itchy ear that needs scratching.

One positive signal is rubbing or stroking the chin and cheek. This indicates interest in or consideration of what you are saying. It doesn't mean the person agrees with you, but it likely means the person is listening.

Crossing the arms over the chest is a sign that you are being closed out. The person is exhibiting a defensive posture and stating, "I don't agree with you, and my crossed arms will protect me." Crossed legs also signal disagreement, particularly in concert with crossed arms. Casually crossed legs (especially when the leg on top is pointing toward you) are a sign of relaxation when the arms and face are also relaxed. If the legs begin to tighten and the crossed leg begins to bounce, the interviewer is getting nervous, not agreeing with you, getting bored, or all of these. Your response should be to slow down, project calmness in your voice, and perhaps shift to another subject if the one you are on seems to be causing the discomfort.

Practice Makes Perfect

The key to turning nonverbal signals into a favorable response lies in first being able to interpret them accurately and rapidly. Next, you must be ready with an alternative direction for your communication to take. This is called "thinking on your feet," and it is a useful skill to cultivate. Your mind must be able to "multitask" or "multiprogram," to borrow some jargon from the computer professionals. This means being able to consider several courses of action, select one or more, and do it—all while carrying on a technical conversation.

This is not easy; it takes a conscious and practiced effort to pull it off. If you can do it, congratulations: You have a formidable weapon in your communications arsenal. If you are one of those people who can only concentrate on one item at a time, I urge you to start developing the habits and skills you need to assess and respond to the environment (in this case, other people's communication signals).

I recall an experience ordering a hamburger at a carryout restaurant. Several people were in line, and the person taking orders also did the cooking. Although the grill was large and spacious, each order was taken and prepared before another was taken. To observe the frustration of those waiting in line while the conscientious fry cook flipped and fussed over each single burger on the giant grill was interesting, to say the least. He ignored suggestions that he put several burgers on the grill and take multiple orders. There was no question that he was doing a good job. Those who got hamburgers proclaimed them to be the best. He didn't even understand why people were getting angry. He failed to pick up on their communication and managed to frustrate them rather than feed them.

The biggest fault of the cook was his inability to do more than one thing at a time. He was focused, but in this case it was not a virtue. Had he observed his customers, listened to their needs, and cooked several hamburgers at the same time, he would have been a success.

SENDING YOUR OWN SIGNALS

Most nonverbal communication and body language is subconscious. People also receive and respond to these signals on the subconscious level. Often while we are hearing one message, we are reacting in a different way—without understanding why.

Once you become aware of nonverbal signals and their meanings, you will begin to understand what others are really telling you. At this point, you can respond by consciously using body language to send messages that are favorable to you. You already do this, but you probably have not considered it in this context. When you dress for an occasion or consciously smile, you are using nonverbal communication to get a message across. You certainly know that if you dressed shabbily for an interview you would create a negative impression and probably not get the job.

There are other aspects of nonverbal communication that can be used to your advantage.

Paralanguage

Paralanguage is vocal expressions outside of the spoken word. It is the qualities of voice tone, inflection, rate, pitch, and volume that support the spoken word. The emphasis placed on a word, in conjunction with the other qualities, can project a variety of meanings.

You should begin listening to how you speak. Try emphasizing different words in a sentence to project different meanings. Try different inflections, rates, and so forth for emphasis. Consciously exercise your paralanguage when speaking in all types of situations, and observe the results. Avoid sounding dramatic or phony; rather, project sincerity in your speech.

Again, I recommend Toastmasters International as an

effective training ground for voice and speech training and a good place to get feedback on the impact of your voice usage.

Body Language

Since most body language is delivered on the subconscious level, you must think about body language and what you want to communicate through its use. Breaking it down into the different areas of your body is one approach to categorizing and understanding it.

Using your Head, Face, and Eyes

Nodding or shaking your head to indicate agreement or disagreement; tilting your head slightly to imply attentiveness or understanding; and bowing or tilting it downward to indicate displeasure, disagreement, or avoidance are just a few of the ways the head can be used to communicate nonverbally.

Facial expression can involve a variety of movements capable of communicating many different messages. One study estimated that the face can make over 250,000 expressions and is the basis for most nonverbal communication.[4] Smiling, frowning, wrinkling the nose, pursing the lips, and displaying a "poker face" all signal meanings. Again, observing the expressions of others and discerning their meanings, then incorporating positive expressions into a conscious communication pattern of your own is the best method of developing this area of body language.

The eyes, with their reputation as "the windows of the soul," have tremendous impact. In American culture, the eyes send many messages.[5] For example, they can indicate when a person wishes to be recognized or left alone. By "catching" another person's eyes, you can send the signal that you want their attention. By averting your eyes from

[4] Ray Birdwhistel, *Kinesics and Context* (Philadelphia: University of Pennsylvania Press, 1970).

[5] Cheryl Hamilton, *Communicating for Results* (Belmont, Calif.: Wadsworth, 1990), p. 130.

theirs, you can tell them you wish to be left alone. You can also keep a conversation moving by continuing eye contact with the other party, or you can signal the end of the communication by breaking eye contact or looking away. Eye contact is used to show interest and attention. By using eye contact while leaning your body slightly forward toward the speaker, you can signal that you think what the speaker is saying is of great interest.

A word of caution: These observations are primarily valid in the middle American majority culture. Foreign cultures or even minority subcultures in U.S. society may place different meanings on nonverbal gestures. For example, staring into another person's eyes is a signal of confrontation or defiance in some cultures; it may even be interpreted as offensive. If you are going to interact with a person from a different cultural background, try to find out how that person interprets different nonverbal signals. Asking such questions of people from another culture is not offensive and is usually appreciated. The fact that you are concerned about their feelings is complimentary and to your credit.

Arms, Legs, and Posture

Sending signals by consciously using our bodies is usually easier than trying to control our eyes and face. As children we were told to "sit up straight," and it's likely we have told our children the same thing. I don't know of anyone who does this because of health reasons. We do it because we know that a person who stands up straight and exhibits good posture is perceived in a more positive manner than a person who stoops over with rounded shoulders.

Body language and posture boil down to the universal perception that if you look confident people will believe that you *are* confident. "Stand up straight and look 'em square in the eye" is the message we give our children. We tell them that because we believe the message that kind of body language sends.

Good posture can be achieved and maintained with a healthy dose of self-consciousness. Remind yourself continually. Steal a look at yourself when you pass a mirror. You're not being vain, but you are building a habit that will ensure that you're not caught off guard sending signals via poor posture.

The handshake is a highly visible body signal. We shake hands consciously, but the manner in which we do it is unconscious. Handshaking is a true art form. The handshake was originally used as a sign of trust to show that you didn't have a weapon in your hand. In U.S. culture today, a firm handshake is the sign of self-confidence. If you have been on the receiving end of a limp handshake, think of how you felt at the time. How did you perceive the person doing the shaking? Your thoughts probably were not very kind. A handshake should be firm, but not bone crushing. You're not in a contest of strength. The best way to take the other person's hand is to grasp it with a firm but steady pressure. Shake it positively, but not in a pump-handle fashion. Linger a moment and allow the person who initiated the handshake to disconnect.

Who offers whose hand first is an issue that hasn't been fully resolved. Purists will quote the etiquette manuals and tell you the initiator should be the senior person, the older person, or the woman if the two parties are a man and a woman. This is a reasonable guideline. However, my advice is to allow the other party about three to five seconds to do the right thing, then you take the initiative. Offering your hand is a courtesy. It is viewed—and with favor—as mildly aggressive.

Gestures with hands and arms should be low-key, positive, and appropriate for the occasion. Gestures such as rubbing your nose, scratching your head, or wringing your hands conjure up meanings that you may or may not want to project. Be alert when you are in a communication situation, and make sure your body language is conveying the message you want to send. Toastmaster training is an excellent way to get instruction and feedback on your gestures.

Touching Others

Physical contact with other people is a sensitive issue. I have already discussed some of the issues surrounding handshakes. Touching others improperly can even be a crime. Some people don't like to be touched. A few years ago, a young man named Fred came into my office seeking my assistance in finding a job. He appeared quite normal when he entered, but when I extended my hand, he jumped back and cried out, "Germs!" He may have had a genuine concern for health and hygiene, but to me he was an oddball. As it turned out, his technical qualifications were adequate, but I never presented him to a client—primarily because of what I viewed as strange behavior. I explained my concerns to him, but he stood fast— a choice that I'm sure will effectively block him from many job choices.

Some forms of touching that should be avoided—at least until you reach a level of intimacy that permits them—are backslapping, hugging, kissing, an arm around the shoulder, and anything that might be interpreted as a sexual advance. I'm not saying that all of these touching actions are necessarily wrong. Under the proper conditions, some of them are quite appropriate. The point here is that you should learn to discern when and how to touch another person in order to elicit a positive reaction.

A Structured and Scientific Approach to Touching. Several years ago, I met a man named Barrie Stern who had an office in a building where I also had an office. His business was giving public seminars on a process he called "Skinetics."[6] Barrie had discovered, analyzed, and studied what all of us know and practice on a subconscious level—that we all enjoy being touched by other people in what we perceive as a positive way. Babies and young children need touching as part of a parental bonding process, and we all benefit from a hug when we feel bad or are hurting emotionally. Studies have even shown that stroking a pet can have the effect of lowering the blood pressure.

Barrie had taken the process of touching a step farther. He had examined its effects on business situations and measured the success achieved through various levels of touching. For example, he taught ten home furnishings salesmen his techniques, then sent them out on sales calls. He instructed them not to touch either the husband or the wife during their first ten calls. Then he told them to touch only

---

[6] Barrie D. Stern, *Skinetics* (Self-published, 1981). Contact Harvey Brody, Delshar Industries, Inc., 300 South Standard Avenue, Santa Ana, CA 92701.

the husband during the next five calls and the wife during the last five. On the next ten calls, the salesmen were to touch both husband and wife. He had the process repeated ten times in order to obtain an adequate sample.

The results were dramatic. When neither party was touched, three sales were made for each ten calls. When either the husband or wife was touched, an average of seven sales were made for each ten calls. When both husband and wife were touched, sales were made nine and one-half times out of every ten calls.

The techniques used were simple—touching the top of the other person's hand with your left hand while shaking hands, brushing the tips of your fingers against the other person's arm, or briefly laying your hand on the other person's while talking.

I do not recommend that you experiment with touching techniques with strangers. Try them with family and friends and observe their reactions.

THE IMPORTANCE OF LISTENING

A wise teacher once told me that God created human beings with one mouth and two ears. Therefore he must have expected us to listen twice as much as we talk. This is a perceptive observation, but it seems to work the other way around. Most people talk much more than they listen. In fact, they seem to be struggling to get words in where they don't belong and continually interrupt the people to whom they are talking.

There are a large number of interpersonal communication training opportunities around, but the majority of them are structured to train people in how to get their message across. To be sure, this is important. However, communication is a two-way street, and if you do not hear and understand what the other person is saying, whatever message you send back is likely to be off its mark.

In their excellent book on people skills, *The Art of Managing People*, Philip Hunsaker and Anthony Alessandra make several strong points supporting the importance of effective listening.[7] They believe that good listening requires objectivity, that it is hard work, and that most people are not effective listeners. They point out that the average person—untrained in listening skills—will remember and understand only 50 percent of a conversation and that this drops to 25 percent 48 hours later.

Most misunderstandings can be traced to poor listening skills, but fortunately there is hope. Listening skills, like other communication skills, can be learned, developed, and applied.

Hunsaker and Alessandra identified four categories of listeners: (1) the nonlistener, (2) the marginal listener, (3) the evaluative listener, and (4) the active listener. At the lowest level, the *nonlistener* not only does not hear what others are saying, but does not even make an effort. Considered by others to be a bore, this person always has the answers, interrupts others as they talk, and is usually disliked. The *marginal listener* is a surface listener. He or she hears the words, but reacts slightly, if at all. This is not a person who does well in a conversation in which ideas and concepts are being discussed. Marginal listeners are worse off than nonlisteners because the people they are communicating with are often fooled into thinking they are being heard when it is not the case. In the case of the nonlistener, the other party can perceive the nonattention and cut the conversation off. With the marginal listener, there is apt to be an angry response when it is discovered that very little communication was getting through. The *evaluative listener* represents the level at which most thoughtful and educated people operate. This person hears and analyzes what is said and understands the content. Where the evaluative listener differs from the *active listener,* who is operating at the most effective level of listening, is that the active listener not only listens to the content of what is said and assesses it logically, but also considers it at an empathetic level. This means the message is also viewed from the point of view of the sender. Being able

---

[7] Philip L. Hunsaker and Anthony J. Alessandra, *The Art of Managing People* (Englewood Cliffs, N.J.: Prentice-Hall, 1980), p. 120.

to put yourself in the shoes of other people and hear why, as well as what, is being said is a worthwhile goal to aim for.

Listening Skills in the Job Search

Listening skills are like most other interpersonal skills—a few basic principles generously salted with common sense and courtesy. Here are a few points to follow. These are put in the context of the job search, but they can be applied to any other communication setting.

  1. *Put yourself in the other person's place.* Consider the employer. If you were looking for a technical professional with your skills, what would you like to hear about? If you listen carefully, the interviewer will tell you. You can trigger this by asking, "What are the qualifications and skills that you are looking for?" Then sit back and listen actively. When it is your turn to talk, you'll be able to answer questions intelligently and in a manner that will best suit the interviewer.

  2. *You can't listen if you're talking.* When you talk, you only say something that you already know. When you listen, you learn what someone else knows. Listening is a growth experience; talking is not. Of course, if you don't say anything, people will not know you know anything. The key here is balance. You are not likely to have to work on the talking part, but it *is* likely that you will need to concentrate and focus on being an effective listener.

  3. *Organize what you hear.* When you read an article or book, it is organized by subject or theme. Usually, the author has divided these into chapters, headings, or some other visual form of organization. When people speak, they do the same thing. They are usually concerned about specific themes or points and speak about those subjects. Even if they ramble or talk around their main points, if you identify their main theme(s), you can cut through the words to the meat. As you listen, ask yourself, "What are the main ideas? What is this person getting at? What is he or she talking about?" Focus on this thought and listen for the answer.

Organize the person's ideas in your mind. You might even want to take notes if the occasion warrants it.

4. *Listen objectively.* This is easier said than done. Asking a human being to assess an idea without reacting emotionally is a nearly impossible request. However, if you are going to be an effective listener, you must eliminate as much emotion and prejudice as you can. Unfortunately, we all have our emotional deaf spots. There are words and ideas that turn us off. Certain words offend us even though it was not the speaker's intent to do so by speaking them. This is especially true if the speaker's theme is a controversial one.

Perhaps a better approach to listening objectively would be to listen empathetically. Hunsaker and Alessandra's "active listener" is able to see the speaker's point of view. This is how you want to be as a listener. You want to be able to understand not only *what* is said but *why* as well.

A caveat for the effective listener is to avoid getting angry. Anger clouds your judgment and distorts your perception of what you hear. This is not fair either to you or the listener. If you wish to react emotionally, do so after you have listened. However, if you do react, never direct your feelings at the speaker. Direct them at what is said.

5. *Focus!* This means concentrating on what is being said. By definition, it means eliminating any distractions that may be going on around the speaker, whether a ringing telephone, street noise, other people, or the speaker's appearance. My wife gets upset with me if she tries to talk with me when I'm reading, working, or watching television. I'm focused on what I'm doing to the exclusion of things that are going on around me. It doesn't mean that I don't want to hear what she has to say; it's just that my focus is on something else.

6. *Give and get feedback.* Feedback is useful in the communication process because it ensures that what is being sent and received is understood. It involves repeating or restating what was said for clarity, as well as asking questions in order to allow speakers to elaborate and expand on their ideas.

7. *Be comfortable—Relax!* If you present a comfortable and at-ease appearance to speakers, they will respond in a similar manner to you. If you are nervous and jumpy, the feeling is contagious. Even though your insides might be in a turmoil, you must concentrate on the appearance of calmness and control.

There are few human activities as nerve wracking as a job search, and the interview is the worst part. Working on your listening skills only during job interviews will not make you a good listener. In fact, it will probably make you appear strange and cost you the job. Being an effective listener is an activity that must become a natural part of your everyday behavior. The only way this can happen is if you practice and work on it continually.

TELEPHONE SKILLS

The telephone was discussed in Chapter 5 as one of the pieces of hardware that can be put to productive use by technical professionals in their job searches. From the point of view of successful interpersonal communications, the telephone will be a mainstay in any job hunting effort.

The interpersonal skills required for effective communication apply to the telephone just as they do to face-to-face contact—only more so! In face-to-face communication, we can take advantage of nonverbal communication (body language). Not being able to see the other party places us (and them) at a disadvantage. There are compensating factors however. Most of my business is conducted on the telephone. Approximately 75 percent of the people I deal with I will never see. My only contact with them is on the telephone. However, in some ways dealing with them on the telephone is even more effective than a personal encounter. The following are a few of the advantages:

1. *Time saving.* Using the telephone or "letting my fingers do the walking" saves me the time and effort of traveling to meet people. This means I have time to talk to other people.

2. *Elimination of "small talk."* "Good morning. How are you? Did you have any problem finding our offices? Would you like a cup of coffee? What would you like in it? Would you care for a tour of our facility?" And so on, and so on. It's a wonder many interviews ever get off the ground. It's not that small talk isn't useful; it provides the lubrication to make the rest of the conversation go smoothly. If an employer launched directly into interview-type questions, he or she would give the impression of being nervous and perhaps a bit pushy.

3. *Elimination of prejudice.* Talking to a person on the telephone eliminates any prejudice that might occur in a face-to-face encounter. An employer client related an experience during an interview in which he felt an unexplainable animosity toward a candidate. Throughout the interview, he sensed that he somehow had met the candidate before, but could not think of where. Wherever it was, it was an unpleasant meeting. After the interview, the employer remembered the occasion. Ten years earlier, his sister had been jilted at the altar and the candidate resembled the bridegroom. Had the employer talked to the candidate on the phone, he would have developed a rapport that was not driven by an erroneous first impression due to the candidate's physical appearance.

I have personally had similar experiences. I have developed positive relationships with candidates on the telephone that might have turned out differently if I had seen them in person. I wish I didn't feel this way. Each of us has prejudices that result in our holding negative views about other people. Intellectually, I know I must judge people on their individual merits and not their appearance. However, attitudes that have been ingrained over a lifetime can affect reactions at the subconscious level. My approach is to tell myself continually that I must judge and evaluate on merit and not appearance.

I know that the goal of our society is tolerance and equality for all. It would be wonderful if this were how society really operated. Unfortunately, we are subject to human failings, and my approach is to try to overcome those failings, not preach about ideal conditions.

SUMMARY

Good people skills are the most important assets that anyone can have. I place their value even above technical knowledge. It is estimated that only 15 percent of involuntary terminations are for technical incompetence while the remaining 85 percent involve some failure of interpersonal relationships. The bottom line is that people skills are necessary complements to the technical skills required for any profession.

Fortunately, like technical skills, people skills can be learned and improved. Communication techniques, listening skills, telephone skills, and other social and interpersonal skills can be learned in formal and informal settings. There are classes, seminars, and books available for those who prefer the formal approach. Organizations such as Toastmasters International and the many associations that exist to support technical professionals offer a less formal opportunity to learn and practice interpersonal skills. No matter what your level of people skills might be, resolve that you will actively work to enhance them, improve on them, and learn new ones. Do it! Your career depends on it!

7

DEVELOPING A TECHNICAL JOB SEARCH NETWORK

When I spoke to the students at California State University at Fullerton about how to find their first technical job, I began by dispelling the commonly held beliefs that résumés and want ads are the ways most people get jobs. The proof was the lack of response to the question, "How many of you who are now working got your jobs by sending a résumé or by answering a want ad?"

When asked directly, "How did you get your present job?", student after student answered, "Through a friend"; "I knew someone at the company"; "Someone told somebody about me"; and so on. Through the personal testimonials of their classmates, these students learned the most valuable lesson about the job search: that networking is the most common and most effective technique that can be used to find a job.

The old saying, "It's not what you know but who you know" is a fact of life. A friend with whom I worked for many years is married to a producer of extravaganzas. She has produced such shows as Superbowl halftimes, the opening ceremonies of the PanAm Games, and numerous television specials. My wife and I were having dinner with her and her husband one evening, and she was sharing with us how much she enjoyed her job and what a great opportunity it was for her. She said she felt fortunate to have such an opportunity because she had no formal training or experience. She told us that people with graduate degrees in related areas are desperately trying to break into the business but can't make the right contacts. Her initial contact was a neighbor who created Disneyland shows and spectaculars, who asked her to work part time as a "gofer." Her responsibilities and knowledge grew until she was able to manage the production of big-time spectaculars. She readily acknowledges that she would never be where she is today if it weren't for the contacts she made through her neighbor. I should make it clear that she is qualified and competent. She literally started at the bottom and grew into her job. Her talent and skills keep her advancing and growing. However, it was who she knew that opened the first door.

Too often, I'm told by technical professionals that skill, experience, and education are the only ingredients necessary for a successful job search. That they are necessary ingredients of job *success*, I will agree. That job seekers can depend on these ingredients alone to find a good job, I doubt.

When technical job seekers find employment, they believe it is primarily because of their technical talents. To a large extent they are correct. However, they fail to take into consideration the reputation they established because of their abilities and the fact that it was the expression of that reputation by people who knew them that was the real reason for getting the job.

SOME QUESTIONS ABOUT NETWORKING

What Is Networking?

Networking is contacting people. The contact may be informal or formal. It may be one at a time or as part of a group. The purpose is to let people know who you are and what you want.

You also want to learn about the people and groups with whom you come in contact: what they do, who they know, and where they are. All of this is important to your networking efforts.

Meeting people and telling them of your career plans is the most effective means of discovering a new opportunity. While it may appear to be informal and casual, it remains the best job search technique available.

Can Technical People Use a Network?

You bet they can! Technical people will find the network even more necessary for a job search than nontechnical people. The reason is that a technical professional is dependent on reputation in an arena where specialized job skills are appreciated. If people who hire in that arena know you and your reputation, you will have opportunities. Of course, in a closed community, your reputation must be good!

Who Are You Trying to Contact in Your Network?

Being selective about who you contact can be dangerous because you don't know who might serve as the spark or catalyst that sets you on the road to your new job. In the search business, we call this sort of prejudging by the term *experting*, and it is not advised. On the other hand, talking to the world can take a long time. You should keep certain objectives regarding the type of people you want to contact in mind. Some people will be able to help you more than others. You need to focus your efforts. Some of the people to include in your network are the following:

1. *People who work for companies where you might like to work.* These people can introduce you to others in the company who can hire you. They may also know what positions are available and who is the hiring authority. By making reference to them when you contact the company, your communication will take on a personal flavor that would be lacking if you were "cold calling" the company.

2. *People who work for companies like those where you might like to work.* There is a subtle difference here. The person with whom you are trying to make contact may be working for a company that is outside of your geographical preference. However, that person might still know people at other companies who could prove useful. Never discount the value of a contact. Even the worst contact will give you the opportunity to practice your interpersonal skills.

3. *Officers (and members) of professional organizations.* To meet these people, you will have to join or attend the meetings of professional organizations. You should be doing this in any case, if only to further your professional knowledge. However, the best reason is to make contacts. Breaking bread with other people is a sure way to move from being a stranger to being an acquaintance. An acquaintance can be a worthwhile contact, but if you make an effort to promote the relationship, this contact may turn into an active participant in your job search.

Most professional organizations have a special interest group for members who are in the process of changing jobs. They also permit you to advertise free of charge in newsletters and bulletins. Take advantage of these "freebies" as well as making unscheduled announcements during the self-introduction periods at meetings of professional organizations.

4. *Alumni contacts.* Education should count for something besides skill and knowledge. One of the best but least worked networks is your alma mater's alumni association. Use it generously and shamelessly. Go to your school's alumni association offices and obtain a list of former graduates who live in the area where you are seeking a job. If their degrees and majors are included, it will help narrow your search for people with similar technical backgrounds.

When you contact someone on the list, use a consultive approach. Don't ask directly for a job, but ask whether they might be able to suggest someone you could contact for help. Asking directly puts people on the spot and may make them uncomfortable. An indirect approach takes away any feelings of obligation. It also opens the door for you to develop a relationship without being shut out by a reply of "No, I don't have anything for you."

5. *Other jobseekers.* People in your technical field who are also looking for work are building their own networks, and both you and they can benefit by an exchange of information. Searching for a job is stressful, and association with others in similar circumstances can also provide emotional support.

CATEGORIES OF NETWORK CONTACTS

There are specific people you will seek out for your network. These fall into the following categories:

1. *Managers and decision makers.* These are people who have the authority to hire you to work in their company. It is important that you target them for contact even though they may not have a current opening. If the chemistry is right, you may find yourself in the enviable position of having a job created to match your special and unique talents.

2. *People who can refer you to a decision maker.* What you know will keep you on the job and moving up, but who you know will open the door to the job. If you don't know the right people, then the next best thing is make contacts with people who do. A question you should ask with every contact is "Do you know any managers in my technical area?"

3. *Contacts who have contacts.* Don't discount the value of any contact. Everybody has contacts, who in turn have contacts, and so on. In the chain will be someone who can put you in touch with potential opportunities.

4. *Mentors and advisors.* These are people who can give you direction concerning your career path and interviewing techniques and can give you valuable advice. They are people you respect who have experience or knowledge in your technical field.

DEVELOPING A NETWORK

While you should target and focus on contacts who can be of greatest benefit in your job search, you should also extend your efforts to include almost everyone you know. Here's a list to get you started:

Relatives. Blood is indeed thicker than water, and you should use family relationships to further your career whenever possible. Getting a job by being related is not immoral or wrong. If you are qualified and can get the job you want because of a family contact, do it.

Family friends. Next to family members, friends of the family make the best contacts. There is a sense of obligation, and you will nearly always get a positive response. Don't be embarrassed to approach these people. It is most likely that they are eager to help you, and they would probably be hurt if you didn't ask.

School acquaintances. Old schoolmates (particularly those who majored in your technical field) are excellent contacts. They will know people in your field who can help you, and they will be able to provide a favorable personal reference.

Alumni associations are a superior contact source. Alumni lists are available that provide names, phone numbers, job titles, and companies. This is a good source for the new graduate. Contacts in the workplace are non-existent for people with no work experience, and the "old school tie" can put you in touch with many successful people.

Teachers and professors. If you were a good student and/ or established a good rapport with your teachers and professors, let them know when you are in the job market. They can put you in contact with people in your field, and their recommendations will carry weight in making the contact.

Neighbors. Many people feel there's a stigma attached to being out of a job or looking for a new opportunity. They keep it to themselves, and when they do change jobs it is usually a surprise to their friends and neighbors. Good job leads come from a variety of contacts, and you should enlist the help of everyone you can. You'll benefit from it, and they'll appreciate the opportunity to help you.

Doctors, dentists, and other professionals. These are people who are in contact with a large number of people. Because they are not in your technical field, their effectiveness as networking contacts is limited. However, don't limit yourself; let everyone with whom you come in contact know you are looking.

Business associates. This should be an obvious contact, but again, many people keep their job search activities to themselves. Get on the phone and tell your business contacts what you are doing.

Recruiters. A sizeable number of positions are secured by professional recruiters. If a recruiter is working on a contingency basis, he or she is motivated to help you find a job. Chapter 12 is devoted to working effectively with recruiters.

Service organizations. Rotary Clubs, Lion's Clubs, and Chambers of Commerce are all sources of contacts who are active and have wide networks of their own.

Fraternal organizations. These are normally thought of as more social than job contacts; however, the wider and more open your network is the greater the probability of your making a useful contact.

Religious groups. These are people with whom you have a common bond. They will be sympathetic and helpful.

Casual contacts. Job leads come from the darndest places. When you meet people on a casual basis, tell them you are looking for a new job opportunity. It's an excellent ice breaker and conversation topic, and it just may unveil a lead.

Good contacts can come from any source, so this list should only be a beginning.

NETWORKING HARDWARE TOOLS

The tools of the job search can be used effectively in building a personal network. Networking is another term for establishing contacts, and whatever tools might help to make those contacts should be used.

The Telephone

Advantages of using a telephone include anonymity, time savings, and the ability to reach places that would be barred to you physically. With a telephone you can reach company CEOs at their desks or at home. You can call at any time of the day or night and anywhere. You can virtually create your network without even leaving home.

Building a Network with a Telephone

1. *Be aggressive.* Don't be afraid to make the call. This may seem to be a needless statement to a person living in a society in which the telephone is viewed as a necessity of life, but the truth is that calling someone you don't know or who might be able to wield a significant influence on your life is intimidating. Talk to telemarketing people and they will tell you stories of people who failed because of this phobia. When it came to job-related phone use, they would freeze, stare at the phone, or find other work to do.

Remember, no one has ever been attacked by someone at the other end of a telephone line. You may get hung up on, cursed, yelled at, or threatened, but they can't get at you. The trick is to avoid these negative responses and make the callee a positive force in your network.

The best advice I ever received in overcoming a reluctance to make a call was to make the call immediately. Don't put it off or write it down on a "to do" list. Do it now! Pick up the phone and call your party. If you don't reach him or her on the first try, that's OK. You've overcome the first hurdle and made the call. You'll call back.

2. *Call at the right time.* Timing is important in any area of endeavor, but in telephone strategies it is critical. The chances are you will not know the person you are calling if you are trying to build a network through initial contacts. A manager is likely to be busiest from 9:30 to 11:30 A.M. and from 1:30 to 4:30 P.M. The manager will be at lunch from 11:30 A.M. to 1:30 P.M., so the best time to reach him or her will be early in the morning or late in the afternoon.

My favorite times for calling an executive are between 8:30 and 9:00 A.M. and between 5:00 and 6:00 P.M. The reason is that the executive is probably in the office and the secretary or receptionist is not yet at work. Also, the executive has not yet become fully committed to a task (morning) or is finishing up for the day (evening).

3. *Make your words count.* You have only a few seconds to get the callee's attention, so you want to choose your words carefully. Do *not* begin with "How are you today?" I have never received a call that began that way from an unknown caller that wasn't a sales pitch. From my own experience I can tell you that it is a turnoff. I can tell the caller's level of telephone expertise from the first ten words that are spoken. Pros identify themselves and state the purpose for the call. An example of how an effective networking call might go would be something like this:

> Mr. Smith, my name is David Moore and I am a computer engineer. I understand you are responsible for research and development at your company. I've been working in R&D at XYZ Corporation for the past five years and am currently looking for a new opportunity. My reason for calling you is to inquire whether you might have such an opportunity in your organization or whether you might be aware of an opportunity elsewhere.

The time required to speak these words is a little over 20 seconds.

There are a variety of responses you might get from the callee. You could get a rude hangup or a job offer. Most likely, if you approach your subject in a courteous, intelligent manner, the response you receive will be the same. If the callee says "I don't have anything for you at this time," don't say "Thank you" and hang up. An effective comeback would be, "I can appreciate that. As an R & D manager, you may be aware of some direction that I might go in my search for an opportunity." Again, you may be rebuffed, but if you don't ask you won't get!

If the callee responds positively, seize the opportunity. If the possibility of a job exists and you are asked to provide information concerning your background, be prepared to deliver a brief presentation. However, before you launch into a speech, find out as much as you can about the job. When a job is mentioned, the first thing you should do is say "Can you tell me something about the position?" Listen carefully. You will hear the elements of the job that are important to the employer. When you reply, focus on those areas. Presenting what *you* believe is important is a serious mistake. Stick to what the employer wants to hear. Suggest that you meet face to face and discuss it further. The face-to-face interview is your goal. No hire will occur without it.

If the response concerns a referral, ask for a name and phone number, then ask whether you can use the callee's name. Immediately after you say "Thank you" and hang up, follow up with a thank-you note. Don't put it off! This is the frosting on the cake, and it will pay dividends.

The Computer

The personal computer is an excellent information manager and can be used to track and record your network. You can list companies, people, positions, referrals, interviews, and follow-ups. The computer and its associated software will allow you to add new names to your list of network contacts and update your existing list. You can include comments and pertinent information about your contacts, select specific items of information, sort them, and print them for future reference.

NETWORKING TECHNIQUES

As you begin the networking process, you will learn much about people. You will meet people who will go out of their way to help you and those who are self-centered and reject your efforts for no apparent reason. The ones who help you will make your day, giving you an emotional lift that will support you in your job search efforts. The best advice I can give you is to look toward the positive contacts and ignore the negative.

A technique used by salespeople to handle rebuffs and negative experiences is to divide their total income by the total number of cold calls they make. If it turns out that each call equals $100, then when they are met with a rude rejection they can hang up, smile, and say "Thank you! That's $100!" We all know that the call is not worth $100, but if the technique works and keeps spirits high, use it.

When you are looking for a job and reaching out to build a network (especially if you are out of work), you will discover who your friends really are. When you are on top, people will reach out to you, seek your advice, and even depend on you for their business interests. When you no longer hold a position that is useful to their interests, many will drop away. Others will be anxious to help you and will not value the relationship on the basis of what it can do for them. These are people to be treasured, and you should remember the lesson when the shoe is on the other foot. Fair-weather friends are not friends at all.

SUMMARY

Remember to include the following in your network:

1. People you know who work for companies where you might consider working or who work for other companies in your industry.

2. People in professional organizations in your technical specialty.

3. Alumni of the college(s) you attended as well as personal contacts from those schools, including faculty.

4. Other job hunters who can be part of both your personal support group and your network.

The types of people who will likely be of greatest service to you in a network are

1. Decision makers and managers—the people who can hire you.

2. People who know or work for a decision maker who can hire you.

3. People who are influential and have contacts who can help you in your job search.

4. Mentors, advisors, and other people whom you respect and who will help and advise you.

When contacting people to build and develop your network, the telephone will likely be your most effective tool. It will allow you to reach many people in a short time, and good time management is essential. In using a telephone, remember to be aggressive but courteous. Track your contacts and organize them on your PC.

If you have any doubts about the effectiveness of networking, conduct your own survey among technical professionals you know and respect. You will find, as I did with the Cal State Fullerton students, that the majority of jobs are obtained through some form of networking.

Networking is an activity that will serve you well in other professional areas. Knowing the right people to contact is an invaluable resource that will enhance your career in more ways than just job changing.

8

INTERVIEWING FOR
THE TECHNICAL
JOB SEARCH

T he key to a successful job search is the interview. What happens during the interview will determine whether there will be a job offer or a rejection. The impression the candidate makes will determine in great measure the size of the monetary offer and the attitude the employer has toward the candidate as the job is begun.

Technical candidates must be especially sensitive to the importance of the interview. I have arranged enough interviews that I can offer an observation that will likely bring disagreement and denials from most technical professionals. Most technical professionals believe that an invitation to an interview is a guarantee of a job offer. They do not approach the interview as the greatest obstacle in their quest for a better opportunity.

Technical professionals also have very little feeling for ascertaining the outcome of a completed interview. Immediately following every interview that I have arranged, I ask candidates their impression of the job and the employer with whom they interviewed. The majority—more than 95 percent—respond not with their observations but with a statement about how well the interview went. They predict that they will get a job offer. Whether this is only wishful thinking or misplaced confidence is a toss-up. Whatever the case, candidates appear to have very little perception regarding their performance or where the interview will actually lead. This is not intended to be a putdown of technical professionals but simply an observation.

INTERVIEWING STRATEGIES

The advice offered here is intended to help you get the best results from a job interview. Much of what is said will apply almost universally in every interview. Other suggestions and strategies will apply only under special circumstances. This is much like the advice given by a coach to a player on an athletic team. When you are in an interview, you are on the playing field and must draw on all your resources for success.

In addition to personal skills, there are strategies and tips learned from others. These strategies and techniques are useful for both first-time and experienced interviewees. What is presented here consists of observations of thousands of interviews, both successful and unsuccessful. The bottom line is that these techniques and strategies work.

Strategies for Scheduling Interviews

Interviews should always be scheduled during your psychological strong time if possible. Since the employer normally controls the time, you can orient yourself to be psychologically "up" for the interview. If possible, try to schedule the interview so the employer will not have to cut it short. For example, unless lunch is on the interview agenda, scheduling an interview at 11:00 A.M. is not a good idea. Also, scheduling an interview near quitting time is a bad practice unless the employer volunteers to stay late. Interviews should be scheduled during working hours except in unusual circumstances. You should strive for the normal and let the other party opt for the unusual, because the unusual requires an explanation and invariably results in an awkward position. Interviewing during working hours lets you see the company in operation. After-hours or weekend interviews give you an incomplete picture of the company in addition to inconveniencing the prospective employer.

Pre-Interview Strategies

The first step in successful interviewing takes place *before* the interview. The face-to-face meeting between prospective employer and candidate is the culmination of a carefully planned and prepared activity. The analogy of the interview and an athletic contest is a good one. Just as an athlete would not consider entering an athletic event without first developing the skills that will offer a reasonable chance of winning, the prospective job seeker should not consider leaping into an interview unless adequate preparation has taken place.

1. *Find out about the company you are going to interview.* Your task is to find out all you can about the company and the person with whom you will be interviewing. You should find out about the company's history, financial position, and products and whatever facts are available about the job you are seeking. Also try to learn about the hiring manager's personality, technical strengths, and idiosyncrasies. If you are working with a search consultant, you have a source who can provide you with excellent background material. You can also use the resources of the public library through publications such as Standard and Poor's *Register of Corporations, Directors and Executives* and Dun and Bradstreet's *Million Dollar Directory.* Annual reports and product brochures provide valuable information and are available from companies for the asking.

2. *Make a dry run.* If possible, try to visit the company a day or two before your interview. This "dry run" will solve the problem of arriving the day of your interview and not being able to find a place to park or locate the personnel or manager's office. It will also give you an opportunity to see the company's environment and observe its employees. You should walk around the building, visit the cafeteria, ask for company literature from the receptionist, and keep your ears and eyes open for clues about company morale, dress codes, degree of tightness or laxness, and physical atmosphere.

3. *Assess and strengthen your interviewing skills.* Interviewing for a job is not a skill most of us exercise on a frequent basis. Because of this, our skills can get rusty. Sharpen and enhance your skills by reading books that give tips on interviewing. Ask your search consultant for advice and, if possible, engage in role playing with someone you respect as being knowledgeable about interviewing. Most important, realize there is always room for improvement and new knowledge regardless of how many interviews you have been on. My experience as a search consultant has taught me to be wary of the candidate who exhibits overconfidence. Such a person nearly always falls short in the interview.

4. *Make the most of the day of the interview.* This is a critical time. You are going to be excited in anticipation of an opportunity that might change your life. You don't want to make any mistakes.

Your greatest concern is time. Give yourself time for everything—getting dressed, driving to the interview, finding the offices, parking, and so forth. If you have a morning interview, eat a good breakfast but do *not* eat in your interview clothes. Your clothes have been cleaned and pressed so that you will look your best, and the last thing you need is a lapful of coffee. Therefore, eat first and dress afterward. When you dress, leave your suit coat off and hang it in your car. Do not put it on until you are heading for the building where your interview will be. You want to appear as sharp as possible, and nothing looks worse than a suit coat that has been sat on in a car.

Plan to arrive at the interview site 30 minutes before the scheduled time. You have to park, walk from the parking area, and locate the office where the interview is to take place. Before announcing your arrival to a receptionist, I suggest you find a restroom. Besides the obvious reasons for visiting a restroom, you want to find a mirror and give yourself a final checkover. Is your hair combed the way you want it? Are your clothes on straight? Are there any smudges on your face? Take a final look, be satisfied, and go have a great interview.

The time has come! You are about to step through the door of the company and interview for a position that may occupy half of your waking hours and provide the income that will allow you to achieve your desired lifestyle.

THE REAL PURPOSE OF INTERVIEWING

Before you take that step, let me ask a question. Why are you going on this interview (or any interview, for that matter)? If you answer the way most people do, you will probably say you want to look the company over to see whether they have what you are looking for. This is an excellent reason for going on an interview, and you definitely want an answer before accepting any position. However, if you come out of the interview and conclude that this is the greatest company and the most ideal job you will ever find and then receive no offer from the company, the reason you gave for interviewing is of little value.

Learning about the company and the job must be a secondary motive for interviewing. Those things provide vital information, but if you are to be successful in an interview, there is a more important motive that must come first. It is this: The primary reason for going on this interview or any other interview is to get a job offer! This is paramount. If you do not get a job offer, the issue of whether or not you'd like to work there is purely academic. When you get an offer, you have the choice of accepting the position or turning it down. Without an offer, your feelings about the company don't matter. You are not in control.

THE PROPER ATTITUDE

What you must achieve is an attitude—an attitude that you will act and speak in a way that will result in your receiving a job offer. Never mind if the job is not what you want. When you get an offer you are in control and can turn the job down. Perhaps the next interview is not what you want either, or the next, or the next. Sooner or later you will have an interview that produces the job you want. If you have approached each interview with the goal of getting an offer in mind, when the right position comes, you will get the offer and the job.

WHAT IT TAKES TO GET AN OFFER

A persistent myth that plagues job seekers is that being qualified will get you the job and help you keep it. Technical professionals are susceptible to this belief because since their careers are driven by their technical skills, they believe they are less dependent than others on interpersonal skills. This is simply not true. Being qualified will help, but it is not the criterion on which you will be hired. Nor is it the reason why you will keep your job.

To prove this, look at the reasons why people are fired. One survey showed that only 15 percent of people fired from technical positions (engineers, computer technicians, etc.) were let go because they were technically incapable of performing their jobs. The reason given for the other 85 percent was that the employees were unable to get along on the job or were otherwise lacking in interpersonal or communication skills.

We've all known technically qualified people who couldn't get or hold a job. We also know people who seem to get the best positions, even though their technical skills are minimal. The reason why this occurs is because employers typically do not hire on the basis of technical strengths. They hire people they like and who they believe will "fit in" with their job environments.

PROJECTING A POSITIVE IMAGE

The key, then, is to project a positive personal image to potential employers. Again, I will emphasize that technical skills and qualifications are important, but the basis of your being hired will be how much the employer likes you. A word of caution is in order here. Employers are not all alike. Some do put greater emphasis on the technical side. However, even these will not hire you if they do not like you or do not believe you want the job they are offering.

How do you present the proper image to an interviewing manager? You certainly don't want to fake a "you" that's not going to be around on a daily basis. You couldn't keep up the act, nor would you want to. What you must do is project the idea to the employer that you are genuinely interested in the position for which you are interviewing. The best measure of interest is enthusiasm, so you must project enthusiasm to ensure a successful interview.

Again, be yourself. We all show enthusiasm in various ways that are easily interpreted by others. Some of us may jump up, wave our arms, and shout. Others may reveal enthusiasm with as little as a raised eyebrow or a twinkle in the eye. However you do it, it should be you. Anything else will be interpreted as phony.

Take your cues from the interviewer. When the interviewer says something that you are interested in, project genuine enthusiasm. Say that you like it. For example, if the interviewer says that the project for which you are being interviewed involves a great deal of state-of-the-art development, you might respond, "That really sounds exciting. I enjoy working on new and challenging projects." This is a basic principle of successful interviewing. If you feel good, say so! Too often, people fail to communicate their feelings. In the case of bad feelings, this may be the proper course of action. If the feelings are positive, the person you are talking to will not know how you feel unless you say so or project your feelings in such a way that they cannot be misunderstood.

Projecting a Positive Image When Feelings Are Negative

The issue gets more complicated when the employer brings up negative or undesirable issues. While you want to demonstrate enthusiasm for the positive things, your responses to negatives must never turn the employer off. One way to handle this is with a technique called *selective response.* Here's an example of how it works. Most technical people are not enthusiastic about writing documentation. If the interviewer were to say something like, "On this project, we are heavily committed to proper documentation," you would never want to respond, "Well, I'm really not too high on doing documentation. Research is more up my alley." You would effectively cut your own throat, and the employer would wind the interview down and politely dismiss you.

A better response—a *selective response*—would be, "I can appreciate the value of good documentation. I've certainly seen the results of poor documentation." The difference is that with a selective response you acknowledge the importance of an issue without expressing like or dislike. If you were asked whether you liked spinach and you hated it, a selective response would be, "Spinach is certainly nutritious and should probably be a part of everyone's diet." You are not admitting to liking or disliking spinach; you are merely agreeing that it is nutritious—a selective and acceptable response.

DEALING WITH NEGATIVE ISSUES

You must address the negative issues at some point before you accept a job. One way is to look at the interview process as having two "positions": *motivation* and *anxiety.* Initially, the job seeker is in the "motivation" position and the employer is in the "anxiety" position. The employer is anxious about whether the candidate is qualified, whether he or she will fit in with the company personality, whether salary needs will be reasonable, and so on. The prospective employee is motivated to overcome these anxieties.

Responses from the job seeker during this phase should be motivational; for example: "I like the job." "How much responsibility would I get?" "When could I start?" Only positive responses should be given during this time. Negatives such as "How much will I get paid?" "How long are the lunch hours?" or "Your plant is sure located in a bad neighborhood!" should be avoided. Employers, on the other hand, have anxieties to deal with. Examples are "How much money do you want?" "Why are you leaving your current job?" or "How much do you know about [the technical area]?"

The roles switch when an offer is made. The employer then becomes "motivated" and the prospective employee can ask the "anxiety" questions. The offer is the key. At that point, the employer has made a commitment to the candidate. The candidate must now make a decision, and hopefully it will be the right one.

DEALING WITH MONEY ISSUES

The issue of money is a pitfall in at least half of all interviews. Both employer and candidate can become so focused on dollars that they lose sight of whether the candidate is right for the job or the company is the right choice for the candidate. For the job seeker, the key to handling money questions during an interview is to *never give the employer an asking price.*

There's a difference between "What salary are you currently making?" and "How much money do you want?" Your current salary is an existing fact; asking about what you expect is speculation. The question "How much salary do you want?" (or any of its derivations) is a prelude to disaster. The employer shouldn't be asking it (at least not yet), and the prospective employee shouldn't be answering it. If you answer this question with a salary figure, you will do one of two things:

1. You may give a number that is less than what the employer is willing to pay. The result is that if you get the job you lose money.

2. You may give a figure that is too high and disqualify yourself from further consideration—even though there are other things about the job that make money less of an issue.

Let's examine the dynamics of these responses more closely. In the first case, you gave a number that was less than the employer was willing to pay. The reason you gave that number is because the employer asked for a figure and you took a guess. Because you stated a salary lower than the one the employer had in mind, you caused the employer to believe you were a bargain and you were hired.

Unfortunately, human labor is the only resource that is capable of reflecting on its own worth. At some point you will discover that other employees who are doing what you do are being paid more. You will either remain quiet and unhappy or approach your employer and request some sort of equity. It's likely the employer will respond to your request by pointing out that it was you who said what salary you expected and therefore you should be satisfied. You will be left with the option of accepting the situation or looking for another job. Neither is acceptable.

In the second instance, you stated a number that was higher than the one the employer had in mind. The employer viewed your salary requirements as being too high, and instead of offering you a lower salary, the decision was to pass on you. A possible reason why the employer didn't offer the lower salary is because of the fear that it might be viewed as an insult. You might not have been insulted, but you'll never know because you didn't get the offer.

What Salary Should You Expect?

A fair question at this point is what salary you should expect. How do employers determine the salary they will offer prospective employees? A number of factors go into this determination, but it boils down to what the marketplace is paying. To put it more simply, you should expect no more than other employees who are performing the tasks you will do and whose skills are similar to yours. You should also expect no less. An employer who agrees to interview you will know your current compensation and that it falls within the range of what the employer would pay—a range that can make the job "attractive" to you.

Handling Inquiries About Money

Unfortunately, many employers continue the practice of asking for salary requirements even though it is to their disadvantage. In the interview, the candidate must respond to the employer's inquiry with tact, but must not state a number. An initial response that will satisfy most employers is, "I'm really more interested in the opportunity the job offers than the starting salary." This may sound a bit hokey, but sincerity where money is concerned is important. You never want to come off sounding greedy. Fair, yes! But greedy, never!

Persistent employers will probably come back with something like "I really need a number to work on. Now, how much do you want?" This is the point at which the faint-of-heart candidate usually caves in. If you are tempted to blurt out a figure, keep the following in mind: If you give a number, you will save the employer (1) *money*—because you'll be under the employer's maximum; or (2) *time*—because you'll be over the employer's maximum and you can be passed over comfortably. In either case, you lose!

Answering "How Much Money Do You Want?"

If you find yourself really pressed to reply to a request for a salary figure, say this:

> Mr. [Employer], you're in a better position than I am to put a salary on the job. You know your needs and you know what you're paying other people who are now doing the same task I would be doing. You also know what you are paying people who have backgrounds and skills similar to mine. I know that whatever *starting salary* you consider offering me will be fair and reasonable, and I'm open to considering any fair and reasonable offer.

Let's examine what you have said. You've thrown the question back to the employer. You have paid him a compliment by acknowledging that he knows more about his needs than you do. You have stated indirectly that you expect to be paid no less than others doing the same work. You have also acknowledged the employer to be fair and reasonable—another compliment. Notice that whenever you use the word *salary,* you say "*starting salary.*" When you say "starting salary," you are implying that any offer you receive will be just that—a starting salary—and that you expect to be reviewed and receive increases consistent with the quality of your work.

If you follow these principles, you will maximize the number of offers you will receive and maximize the salary amounts of those offers.

Since much of the leverage you have concerning salary is in your current salary, it follows that the higher the starting salary, the greater your salary will be over your work life. When you look for a job in the future, you will be at a higher salary and therefore will command a higher salary, and so on. Depending on where you are in your career and how many years you have before you retire, this information can be valuable. Earning an additional $50,000 to $100,000 during your work life would not be unusual.

SUMMARY

The pivotal point of a successful job search is the face-to-face interview with the person who can hire you. Scheduling that interview is the primary goal of the job seeker, since no job offer will be tendered unless an interview takes place.

The timing of interviews is important; the best times are mid-morning or mid-afternoon. Avoid after-hours interviews if possible, because they do not allow you to see the organization in operation. Breakfast, lunch, or dinner interviews allow you to get to know the manager better from a social point of view, but they should be linked to an interview at the place where you will work.

Do your homework prior to the interview. Visit the library and refer to business publications for information on the company, and inquire into your network for people who might know the person with whom you will be interviewing. If you have time, visit the company the day before your interview and look it over.

On the day of your interview, give yourself plenty of time. Arrive 30 minutes before your scheduled interview time.

Keep in mind that your goal in interviewing is to generate a job offer. Only if you receive a job offer are you truly in control.

While technical competence is important, in the interview situation it is considered a given. If technical competence is equal, the deciding factors will be your ability to communicate your competence for the job and the personal impression that you make. Project enthusiasm and a positive attitude while avoiding negative issues. Avoid discussions about salary and money, and steer the conversation back to your interest in the job.

Whether you are going on your first interview or you're an old hand, being prepared will pay off. Read this chapter again and again, particularly just prior to an interview. Read other books on interviewing (a recommended list is provided at the end of the book). Get other points of view and adapt them to your personal style. Conduct practice interviews and ask for straight-from-the-shoulder criticism. Get feedback from your interviews. Don't be discouraged by temporary failures. Keep trying!

In the job search business, there are few absolutes. However, the axiom that everybody who looks for work finds work is true. I can't tell you how many interviews it will take or how long. I can only tell you that it *will* happen.

CHAPTER

9

MAKING AN IMPRESSION DURING THE INTERVIEW

The Importance of Dressing Properly

There is an old saying that you'll never have a second chance to make a good first impression. It may be a cliché, but it is true. The first time a candidate meets an employer is usually when they meet for the first interview. This is the first impression that is made, and also the most lasting. The impression is made before any words are spoken. When I debrief an employer following an interview and the first comments I hear are "The candidate looked like a clown" or "Doesn't she know enough not to wear blue jeans to an interview?" it tells me that the candidate never had the opportunity to demonstrate technical competence.

The argument that employers hire technically qualified candidates and not good dressers is true. Dressing well will

162

not guarantee a job, but ignoring the effect of dressing appropriately is an invitation to failure.

In his bestselling book, *Dress for Success* (latest version *The New Dress for Success*) (Warner, 1988), John T. Molloy presents overwhelming evidence that clothing can be used to influence and impress. This book is an excellent reference for anyone desiring to learn more about how clothes can affect the perceptions other people have of us. Also recommended is *The Woman's Dress for Success Book* (Warner, 1977) by the same author.

John T. Molloy's two books contain excellent advice, and I consider them absolute musts as tools for guiding your job search and career. They go beyond merely being good advice on dressing properly. Molloy offers insight concerning clothing purchase, style, and the social and psychological impact of clothing.

If at this point you are thinking that I am overselling the importance of dressing properly, allow me to interject this thought: I have seen enough intelligent, highly qualified, and well-educated technical professionals who dress like hayseeds to last a lifetime. Plaid shirts with neckties hanging three inches above the belt, white socks with black "marching band" shoes, and plastic pocket protectors with a row of pens and pencils are a few examples of the looks I've seen on otherwise sharp professionals. And so you won't think I'm picking on male professionals, I'll put it on the record that I've seen women who look just as frumpy. Blue jeans, sweatshirts, excessive makeup, and unkempt hair won't do much to advance their careers. Wearing expensive clothes won't do the trick either. If the clothes are selected without consideration for the impact they will make or if the fit is improper, the money they cost is wasted.

A study at Fairleigh Dickenson University in New Jersey showed that dress has an effect not only on getting a job, but also on the amount of money offered as salary. Employers were shown pictures of several women as they would normally dress for a job interview, and then after their hair was styled and they were wearing clothing suggested by fashion advisors. The employers stated they would offer salaries 8 to 10 percent higher to the women dressed by professionals.

THE FIRST IMPRESSION

The image you present to a prospective employer when you meet for the first time will be the one the employer will remember the longest. The idea that people judge you for who you are and not what you wear is a marvelous sentiment, and it has truth in it. However, the only "you" the employer will know for the first few minutes after you meet is the one he or she sees. After the interviewer gets to know you, what you wear will have less importance. For the interview, you can't afford to take chances.

A male candidate should wear a dark blue or gray suit, a plain white or light blue long-sleeved dress shirt, a conservative necktie (dark red is recommended), black dress shoes, and black socks. A conservative haircut is suggested—and no beard. If you do wear a beard or mustache, neat and well-groomed are the watchwords.

A woman should also keep her dress conservative. A jacketed suit dress, medium-heeled shoes, a conservative hairstyle, and modest jewelry are recommended. Studies indicate that men tend to treat women in a manner consistent with their style of dress. Women in hiring positions have been found to respond the same way to clothing styles. If a woman dresses in a frilly blouse and a cute "little girl" hairdo, she will be treated with less respect than if she were wearing conservative business clothing.

A Few "Don'ts"

- Don't wear casual clothing to an interview. This includes open-neck shirts, sports attire, sport jackets, blue jeans, and the like.

- Don't wear soiled or wrinkled clothing. Always appear fresh and crisp.

- Don't wear unshined shoes. A person who is careless about footwear is probably careless about other things.

- Don't be extreme or garish in your dress. The key to dressing for an interview is to be conservative. If you must "do your thing," do it after you have the job.

MOLLOY'S ADVICE FOR WOMEN

John T. Molloy believes that women dress not for business success, but for failure, because of three basic mistakes.[1] First, their clothing choices are influenced by the fashion industry; second, their self-perception is primarily that of a sex object; and third, their choice of clothing is driven by their socioeconomic backgrounds.

This may appear to be the biased opinion of a male chauvinist, but Molloy's conclusions are based on research, not opinion. His research is based on reactions to various images projected by women as they dress in a variety of styles in various business settings. The image that a woman in business wants is one that commands respect from both men and other women, and she does not have to give up her femininity in order to achieve it.

One suggestion offered by Molloy is that women should adopt a recognizable "business uniform."[2] Unlike men, whose dark blue or gray suits, white shirts, and conservative ties make up their accepted "uniform," women do not have a universally accepted outfit. Molloy's recommendation is that women's "uniform" be a dark-skirted suit with a contrasting blouse. This will give them the look of authority they need to succeed and project a competent image in business. He contends that women must wear this outfit in their professional lives so that it will be recognized for what it is.

I agree with Molloy, but I must point out that it will not be easy for women in business to establish a uniform look because it is currently not generally accepted. Men, on the other hand, have enjoyed a uniform look for decades.

Women are now accepted as business and technical professionals. They are no longer novelties. It was not too many years ago when mention of a female engineer was cause for wonder. Now it is normal. While there may be disagreement as to whether women have achieved equality with men in the

---

[1] John T. Molloy, *The Woman's Dress for Success Book* (Warner, 1977), p. 16.

[2] Ibid, p. 34.

workplace, there is no argument that they are there to stay. The use of clothing by women to achieve an authoritative, businesslike, and respectful image will give them equal footing with their male counterparts.

A woman looking for work should seek any edge she can get. This is especially true in the technical workplace, which is still dominated by men and viewed by many (employers included) as a man's world.

A PERSONAL EXPERIENCE

An experience I had involving clothing and its impact on others may help convince you of the necessity for dressing properly to advance your career. Several years ago, as I was preparing to leave the Marine Corps and enter civilian life, I enrolled in a course offered at the Pentagon by Catholic University in Washington, D.C. The course was titled "Strategies of Career Transition," and its purpose was to equip the students to find a job.

One class devoted a full evening to a guest speaker who was a clothing consultant representing a local clothing chain. He was especially well qualified, having been the consultant to four presidents of the United States. The information he offered was directed mostly at men, but the principles applied equally to women.

I thought I knew how to dress properly, but the emphasis on wearing high-quality dark blue and gray suits with solid white shirts and maroon ties in traditional patterns impressed me. He told of experiments in which men wearing the recommended dress would approach a building entrance and people would step aside and even open the door for them. When the same people wore casual clothing, people at the door pushed ahead of them and, in some cases, physically shoved them aside.

Since I was about to embark on my own job search, the following week I bought an outfit as recommended by the consultant, complete with accessories—a dark blue suit, long-sleeved white dress shirt, silk tie, and black dress shoes.

After dressing in my new clothes, I headed for a large shopping mall and tried my own experiment. I would head for a door, timing my arrival to coincide with that of another person. Just as predicted, the person would yield to me. I also would walk toward other people to see whether they would step out of the way. They did. To wrap up my experiment, I went into several shops and discovered that the clerks gave me immediate attention.

The next day I dressed casually and repeated the experiment. My clothes were a pair of corduroy slacks and a crew neck sweater. They were good-quality clothes and could not be considered the least bit shabby. The response was amazing—at least to me. People at the doors pushed ahead of me, and, although no one got physical with me, there was no deference and certainly no respect. When I walked toward people, many would actually run into me rather than step aside. In the same stores where the day before I received immediate service, I was literally ignored.

My personal experience with the power of clothing made me a believer. I am telling you that it works, and you should use this knowledge to your advantage in your job search and your career. Remember, being well dressed for an interview will not guarantee a job, but it will never hurt. Don't take a chance where your future is concerned.

A REQUEST FROM THE AUTHOR

I have made myself clear concerning how I feel about the importance of appearance and the part dressing properly plays in it. It *is* important, and I found out for myself just how much. Now I'm going to ask you to do the same. Look at the people you admire. While some of them may be casual dressers, it is likely that they are conscious about their appearance and work to present a favorable image. Look at the people you consider successful. It's not necessary that you know them. They may be people in your profession, people in public life, television personalities, or anyone else. The only requirement is that you consider them successful for some reason. Again, I'm betting that they present an impressive personal appearance.

Now I want to encourage you to look at your own appearance and ask yourself if these people were looking at you, what conclusion they would make about you. Would they consider you as a person who presented a favorable and impressive image or as a turnoff who failed to leave any impression at all?

A PLAN OF ACTION

Being told success stories and the value of dressing for success may impress you. It may even move you to say, "I believe that image and dressing are important to career success." Reading books like those of John Molloy may give you additional motivation since they provide details about what clothes to wear for specific effects. But regardless of how convinced you are that these things can improve your chances of getting a job and enhancing your career, they will be worthless unless you act on them.

For Men

If you are a man, I propose that you take the following action: Collect at least a dozen annual reports from Fortune 500 companies. Look at the pictures of the chief executive officers or company presidents. Select three who are dressed conservatively and then pick the one you'd like to look like. This is probably going to be difficult, because these people are probably all wearing the "uniform" (i.e., dark blue suit, white shirt, and conservative necktie). Go to a high-quality clothing store, ask for the manager, and tell him that you are trying to achieve an image like that of the gentleman in the annual report. If you have selected a good clothing store, the manager will understand. He will probably turn you over to an experienced salesperson who will give you good advice and help you reach your goal.

For Women

The plan for women is similar. Because there are fewer female CEOs, annual reports featuring women may be harder to find, but they are available. However, the accepted business "uniform" for women is more varied and not as well established as it is for men, and women's clothing stores are not as attuned to business dress as those catering to men. They tend to focus more on style and current fashions than on business image. There are stores that can give you excellent guidance, but you may have to look a little harder than men do. It will be well worth the investment of your time.

For Both

After you have purchased a basic wardrobe, begin to wear it in your work environment and alternate it with your old work clothes. Observe the way other people respond to you. Is it different from when you wore your usual dress? If you go on an interview, wear your new image and consider the response compared to what you may have received in the past.

I believe you will find that a new world has opened up for you. Try it for yourself and see. At the very least, you will have a new wardrobe and some meaningful observations. My own involvement in similar experiments leads me to believe that you will have a pleasant and rewarding experience.

SUMMARY

A sharp, businesslike appearance makes a good first impression. Start developing that appearance by buying John T. Molloy's *The New Dress for Success* (Warner, 1988) if you're a man and *The Woman's Dress for Success Book* (Warner, 1977) if you're a woman.

If one word were chosen to describe how applicants or candidates should dress for interviews, it would be *conservatively.* Men should wear a dark blue or gray suit, plain white or light blue dress shirt, and a conservative necktie (in style). Women should wear a jacketed suit dress (gray is recommended) with equally conservative accessories.

Remember, this is the first impression you are making on a person for whom you may be working for years. You want your first meeting to be recalled with favor.

10

EVALUATING THE TECHNICAL JOB

F inding and landing a job is a major effort—particularly if it's the right job. But how do you know? How do you evaluate the merits of a job offer? Is it a good career move? Will it fulfill your career goals?

Keeping up with what's happening in the marketplace and the technology of your profession is critical to your career. Technical development in today's world advances rapidly. A technical professional can't afford to make a mistake or get trapped in a dead end situation.

I recall a cartoon showing two well-dressed men walking through a park. A shabby, down-on-his-luck fellow was sitting on a park bench looking very dejected. One of the well-dressed types turned to the other and remarked, "A real shame. Smith over there was a top computer specialist. Went on three weeks' vacation and fell so far behind in his field, he couldn't catch up!" This may be a joke, but there's a ring of truth to it. Three weeks may not put you out of the running in your field, but two or three years in the wrong job can be very damaging.

Several issues are important to the technical professional

who wants to keep ahead of the career game. These include establishing decision criteria for accepting or rejecting potential job offers and properly assessing the job market; dealing with financial issues; planning career moves and objectives; evaluating job and technical growth potential; and weighing educational concerns, training opportunities, and geographical matters.

WHAT IS A JOB?

Before considering the merits of various career choices, it is appropriate to define that entity called a *job*. A job is many things. It is the means by which we achieve economic independence; the way we provide sustenance for ourselves and our families; the way we contribute to society; and the way we achieve personal satisfaction and self-esteem.

We work at our jobs more hours than we spend in any other endeavor, including family activities. A job is the most structured activity in a person's life, and if that person is unhappy in it, he or she will most certainly be unhappy in the other areas of life. Conversely, when a person is happy in work, that happiness most likely extends to the other parts of his or her life.

There are many things in life that we value and are important to our personal, social, economic, and spiritual well-being. If we were asked to rank these things in their order of importance, we probably would not be able to do so without difficulty. There are different factors impacting on each area that would make it appear more important than any other.

Jobs would probably be at or near the top of the list. We could rightfully argue that family, religious faith, or duty to country should come first, but only jobs provide economic support for the other things we hold valuable. It is for this reason that people usually evaluate job opportunities in economic terms rather than by noneconomic or intangible criteria.

When a job is offered, the issue usually brought up first is how much it pays. While the economic benefits of a job *are* important, it is equally vital that the offer be viewed from many other perspectives.

ASSESSING THE JOB OFFER

When most people think of an offer, the first question they ask is "How much is it?" Although an offer is associated with salary, it also consists of other, even more important ingredients. Too often money masks the issues that really make a job worth considering. Money is more of a detractor than an attractor. Too much or too little of it can turn a candidate's head from the concerns that make a job truly worth having.

Besides money, an offer is made up of the ingredients described in the following paragraphs.

What You Will Be Doing

If the job is interesting and challenging, it can be compared favorably with other job offers and your current job. Your current job is often overlooked when considering a new position. Actually, it should be the benchmark against which other opportunities are measured. What you will be doing determines whether the job will be interesting and enjoyable, has a promising career path, and is a preferable alternative to your current job.

The Technology Where You Will Be Working

A technical professional should seek a job that is satisfying and challenging, but there is an additional dimension not found in most other jobs. This is the need to gain ongoing experience and keep current in state-of-the-art technology.

The technology where you work will define your experience. If that technology is the latest and most challenging, your experience will be in demand. If the technology is old or narrow and specialized, you may find yourself in a dead end situation with experience no one can use.

Your Job Title

The job title is often thought of as an ego trip, and the comment is heard that title means very little. I have listened to the concerns of too many technical professionals to believe that job titles are not important. A step up to "senior," "principal," or "consulting" engineer, analyst, or technician is a visible indication that you are moving up in your career. Even if the money is the same, a step up in responsibility as demonstrated by a change in job titles is not a lateral move.

Where the Job Will Be Located

The location of the job is not related to its technical side, but it certainly has an impact on job satisfaction. Anyone who has endured an hour or more one way on a commute can attest to the importance of having a job that's close to home. Geography is usually not the driving force behind a job choice, but it is a factor.

Your concern with job location may manifest itself in several ways. It may be important to find a job closer to home, or perhaps closer to relatives or friends. Perhaps you would like a job that's close to recreational facilities or in an area where the weather is more to your liking. Most people would choose a job closer to home if all other things were equal.

A more professional reason for making geography a priority is to move to a location where your technical skills will be in greater demand or where the opportunity for work is more promising.

Who You Will Be Working For

Taking a job because of the boss may sound a bit odd. However, I have interviewed several thousand job seekers over the years, and one of the first questions I ask is why they want to leave their current job. If you asked this question of managers, their answer would most likely be "money." The two answers I receive almost universally are "limited technical growth or career opportunity" and "personal differences with management." The latter really means "I'm not getting along with my boss."

A company's reputation as a good place to work can usually be traced back to the way individual managers treat their employees. In fact, a single company may receive mixed reviews depending on the people you talk to and what their opinion is concerning their boss. The reality is that who you work for can mean the difference between your job being a pleasure or a misery.

Where the Job Will Take You

This means the career path and growth opportunities offered by the job. You must look beyond the immediate job and evaluate not only what it offers you now but where it will take you. A job that pays more than others offered may not be the best choice. If the job has no future or no promotion possibilities, it is probably a poor choice. If the only move on the career path is the job held by the boss, who has held that position for several years and shows no signs of leaving, your chances of moving up are slight.

Too often, a job is accepted because it offers an escape from what is perceived as an undesirable current job. When I first entered the search business, I was told that there were only two perfect jobs you could ever have: the one you had before the one you have now and the next one you're going to have. Jumping from a frying pan into a fire, as the old cliché goes, is not a good idea. A job should offer you an opportunity to grow in your technical abilities and be a means to achieving your career goals.

A JOB OFFER *IS* THE MONEY!

The job offer is all the things I've just mentioned. However, I do not want to imply that money is not important. Money is the measure by which employers gauge employees' worth, and it is obviously better to be paid well. The only people who work for free are independently wealthy, volunteers with other means of support, or fools!

The amount of money a job pays is an indication of the value of that job and the person holding it. A job requiring extensive training and experience will pay more than a job for which the qualifications are few and which has many people available who are capable of performing it.

While money should never be the only criterion by which a job is evaluated, it will always be considered in the equation in some form. The important consideration is to put money into the proper perspective with the other criteria that are important to you.

OTHER EVALUATION CRITERIA

Education

There are few assets as valuable to a technical professional as education. You may hear the argument that experience is more valuable, but there are few, if any, technical positions that do not require education or training of some sort before the work can be done. Thus, a major criterion to consider with any job is education.

This is viewed from two perspectives. First is the value the prospective employer places on education. If education is highly prized and the employer believes that it is a key to job success, the job should be regarded more highly. As a technical professional, you have worked hard to get your education. If you have gone through a degree program, you have demonstrated discipline over a long period of time in order to fulfill prerequisites for the degree. If the employer believes that education is of little value, your education and the efforts you put into getting it are also going to be viewed in that manner. You want a job that places a high value on your hard-earned education.

The second perspective is whether or not the prospective employer values education enough to provide financial support for you to either complete or advance your schooling. The cost of degree programs and other technical training makes this a valuable benefit in any job offer.

When considering this criterion, you should know whether *all* education is paid for by the employer or it is limited in some way. For example, some employers will pay only for education that is relevant to a specific job. They may pay for technical design courses if you are an engineer, but will not pay for mathematics courses that are required for a degree. Some will pay only upon course completion, while others prorate the amount paid by the grades you receive in the course.

Another important type of education is technical (noncollege) education. I know a senior communications engineer who will not accept or even interview for a position unless the prospective employer agrees to fund his technical education. He also insists on being sent to conferences and funded for memberships in professional societies. This eliminates employers who do not value technical education, and it settles up front the amount of technical education he can expect. I will add that every employer this person has worked for has benefited by the training he has received. An employer who values and provides technical training is a real plus in any position evaluation.

Benefits and Perquisites

I have placed the issue of benefits last because that is where I believe they should be considered in the evaluation equation. Benefits and perquisites include such things as medical insurance and care, dental care, vacation, company cars, and the like. These are part of a compensation package and are worth money to the job hunter. However, if the job is not right and does not enhance the candidate's career and technical growth, whatever form the compensation might take will not offset what the technical professional will be sacrificing. The bottom line is to consider the technical growth and advancement first, then the compensation package.

SUMMARY

Evaluation of a job is an evaluation of the future. A job decision must be considered carefully and viewed primarily from the perspective of how it will advance your career. Money is important, but it must be secondary to where the job will take you technically. An important observation is that if you concern yourself with the technical side of the position first, you will make an investment in your future that will provide you with the income you desire and deserve down the road.

11

LEGAL RIGHTS OF THE TECHNICAL JOB SEEKER

This is a chapter that should not have to be written. The thought that any current or prospective employer would knowingly or unknowingly violate the legal rights of an employee or job candidate is repugnant to me. The real world, however, is not the nice place I would like it to be. There are volumes of laws and regulations pertaining to the rights of employees, equal opportunity employment, job safety, and unemployment. Knowledge about these rights is widespread, and there are ongoing public education efforts as well as organizational information programs aimed at offsetting and preventing violations. In spite of these efforts, however, horror stories abound of employees and job seekers who have been affected and injured by both intentional and nonintentional violations.

The real villain, I believe, is ignorance, primarily on the part of the employee or job seeker. An employer who knowingly breaks the law and causes harm to someone should be hammered to the full extent of the law. An employer who unwittingly violates someone's rights can also be held accountable and penalized under the law. However, the individual who allows someone to infringe on his or her rights is equally at fault—and is also the one with the most to lose.

I should state at the outset of this discussion on the rights of job seekers that I am not an attorney. Any discussion of law or rights should be considered as information only and not construed to be legal advice. If a situation arises in which you believe that your rights have been violated or a question of law is at issue, you should contact an attorney.

WHAT TO DO IF YOU HAVE A LEGAL PROBLEM

What can the individual do to protect against unfair or illegal treatment in job situations? Fortunately, there are several courses of action.

1. *Learn the laws, regulations, and statutes pertaining to your job rights.* This is easier to say than do. The U.S. government and the governments of the various states have, in their efforts to protect and care for us, enmeshed us in a tangle of laws that even the courts have difficulty dealing with. If the legislatures, courts, and lawyers can't make sense of the laws, then what chance does the humble layman have?

The answer is to read and question. The personnel offices of most companies have copies of all laws relating to the rights of workers. If the company is of any size, it has a lawyer on staff or on retainer for the purpose of dealing with workers' rights as well as other legal issues. Ask to see the laws. In some cases, summaries of workers' rights laws must be posted. Ask direct questions to employee and industrial relations representatives about your rights. Understand, however, that company representatives and lawyers are representing the interests of the company, and the advice you receive will likely be slanted in favor of the company.

Numerous books have been written on workers' rights. One excellent book is *Your Rights At Work*, by Darien Mc-Whirter (Wiley, 1989). Mr. McWhirter is an employment attorney and offers an overview of the laws affecting the rights of workers. Included are case summaries and examples couched in layman's language. The book is particularly valuable because it is written from the worker's point of view.

2. *Contact an attorney.* Lawyers generally get a bad rap, and I'm sorry to say many deserve it. But when you're in legal trouble, they can be your best ally. They understand the rules and how to play in an arena where you would otherwise be completely vulnerable.

Finding a good attorney is the first step. There are over 700,000 attorneys in the United States, and the number is growing. With that many to choose from, finding a good attorney would appear to be a simple task. However, not every attorney is a specialist in employment or labor law, and once you have found one who has that kind of expertise and experience, you're still not guaranteed that the lawyer is a good one. Since half the practicing attorneys graduated in the lower half of their classes, a better measure of their true worth is favorable references. Someone who has experienced a similar experience can tell you who will do a good job for you and who will not.

Good chemistry between you and your attorney is a must. The attorney must believe in you, like you, and be willing to work for you. Operating style is also essential. The lawyer who acts as if talking to you or meeting with you is an inconvenience or a nuisance is a loser. Worse is the lawyer who projects this image and then puts you on a meter and charges you for every minute of time. My personal preference is the "junk-yard-dog" style of lawyer. This person is assertive, knows the business, loves a good scrap, and is willing to lay it on the line for your case. This is also the type of lawyer who will tell you if your case is weak and you should settle or back out.

Lawyers are expensive. Many will demand a retainer or fee up front and then hourly charges. You want to find one who meets the experience and personality qualifications and is willing to take your case on contingency. This means the lawyer gets paid if you win your case. If you must pay for the lawyer's time, determine what you will get for your money. Don't let the lawyer intimidate you. You are the customer. You are paying the money, and you will call the shots. The lawyer is only a professional advisor who can represent your interests in court. Get your money's worth.

Be up front with your lawyer. Don't leave out details that might appear unfavorable to your position. Only if the lawyer is aware of these facts can he or she prepare a proper case in your favor. The worst position you can place your lawyer in is to surprise him or her with facts that you could have provided. Actually, it won't be the lawyer that is in a bad position, it will be you.

3. *Contact federal and state agencies.* There are numerous federal, state, and local agencies that administer the laws pertaining to workers' rights. When you know or suspect that a law has been violated, one way to find out which agency has jurisdiction over your case is to call your congressional or state representative. The phone numbers of their local offices are listed in the telephone directory, and they can direct you to the right office. If you happen to get a staff worker who can't seem to help you, don't give up. Ask to speak to another person in the office or write a letter directly to the representative.

If you don't get satisfaction from the agency, there are several alternatives you can try. First, understand that federal and state agencies are usually overworked and undermanned. You may also be dealing with a bureaucrat or clerk whose primary motivation is moving paper, not solving problems. Fortunately, most public servants are sincere people. They just have too much to do. Explain your situation and ask what laws apply and whether you have a case. Then ask what courses of action are available to you and what the next step should be. If the person you're talking to doesn't appear to be helping, ask to speak to the supervisor. Be courteous, calm, logical, and direct. Don't sound threatening or excitable. Each day government agencies are besieged with calls, and many of them are from unreasonable kooks. You want to present yourself as someone whose case deserves attention. It may be that you have no case or that the circumstances do not constitute a violation of the law.

4. *If the incident occurs on your current job, go to your company's industrial relations representative.* This should probably be your first step before taking your grievance outside the company. Talking to the boss or the boss's designated representative gives the company the opportunity to resolve the issue. Actually, most employers would prefer to handle grievances this way. If you are rebuffed, then consider one of the other courses of action. If your employer tells you that you don't have a case, don't be put off. Seek a second opinion outside the company.

LAWS AFFECTING THE JOB SEEKER

There are numerous laws and regulations that have bearing on your rights as a job hunter. Because laws change and new laws are passed, I won't attempt to cover every law. Also, state laws vary. Since my state is California, any discussion of state laws will be in reference to California. You should check the specific laws, codes, and regulations of your own state.

Equal Employment Opportunity Legislation

The following laws lay the foundation for the legal requirements that must be met in order to comply with equal employment opportunity legislation.

Title VII of the 1964 Civil Rights Act

Title VII is administered and enforced by the federal Equal Employment Opportunity Commission (EEOC). The law forbids all discrimination in employment because of color, race, ancestry, creed, marital status, physical disability, sex, or national origin. It covers all terms and conditions of employment and holds the employer responsible for any discrimination going on within the employer's organization. The law is applicable to all employers with 15 or more employees for at least 20 weeks during the year. The main section of Title VII reads as follows:

(A) It shall be an unlawful employment practice for an employer:

(1) to fail or refuse to hire or to discharge any individual, or otherwise to discriminate against any individual with respect

to his compensation, terms, conditions, or privileges of employment, because of such individual's race, color, religion, sex or national origin, or

(2) to limit, segregate, or classify his employees or applicants for employment in way which would deprive or tend to deprive any individual of employment opportunities or otherwise adversely affect his status as an employee, because of such individual's race, color, religion, sex or national origin. (42 U.S.C. sec. 2000e-2)

The Equal Pay Act of 1963

The Equal Pay Act is a part of the Fair Labor Standards Act and applies to all employers and employees covered by that legislation. It also covers employers who have too few employees (less than 15) to be covered by Title VII. It is also applicable to executives, outside salespeople, administrative personnel, and professionals. It forbids pay differentials based on sex and is enforced by the Wage and Hour Division of the Department of Labor. Here is the pertinent portion of the law:

> Employers are prohibited from discriminating between employees on the basis of sex by paying wages to employees in such establishment at a rate at which he pays wages to employees of the opposite sex for equal work on jobs the performance of which requires equal skill, effort, and responsibility, and which are performed under similar working conditions, except where such payment is made pursuant to (1) a seniority system; (2) a merit system; (3) a system which measures earnings by quantity or quality of production; or (4) a differential based on any other factor other than sex. (29 U.S.C. sec. 206(d)(1))

The issue of equal pay on the surface appears to be cut and dried. However, it raises various complex and variable issues. For an excellent discussion of these issues, refer to the chapter on sex discrimination in Dennis McWhirter's book, *Your Rights At Work* (Wiley, 1989).

The Age Discrimination in Employment Act

This law covers the same employees covered by Title VII. It is enforced by the Wage and Hour Division of the Department of Labor and bans discrimination against anyone 40 years of age or over. Although the federal law applies to employers with 20 or more employees, most states have similar laws that apply to employers with fewer employees. The law applies not only to discrimination because of age in hiring, but also to terminations, pay, hours, and working conditions.

Executive Order 11246

This order applies to employers who have contracts or subcontracts of more than $10,000 with the federal government. It also applies to contractors and subcontractors who are performing construction projects that are in any part financed by federal funds. The order requires that every contract contain a clause against discrimination because of sex, religion, color, race, or national origin.

The California Fair Employment Practice Act

This is a California law that bans job discrimination on the basis of sex, age, marital status, medical condition, physical disability, ancestry, national origin, color, religious creed, or race. It also has provisions for equal pay and access to all personnel records. Other states have similar laws that supplement the federal laws and in most cases are more specific and tougher.

Issues Surrounding Medical Conditions

Discrimination on the basis of medical condition is a touchy and controversial issue. As a result of a Supreme Court decision in 1987, persons with diseases were determined to be disabled as defined in The Rehabilitation Act of 1973. This act establishes a person with a disability to be "any person who (a) has a physical or mental impairment, which substantially limits one or more of such person's major life activities,

(b) has a record of such an impairment, or (c) is regarded as having such an impairment." (29 U.S.C § 706(6)).

According to other federal statutes, people with diseases such as cancer are also covered, as are people with epilepsy, learning disabilities, emotional problems, and obesity.

Drug and Alcohol Addictions

In their civil rights laws, many states have declared that persons addicted to alcohol and other narcotics are considered to have disabilities.

The various federal and state laws pertaining to drug testing and termination because of drug and alcohol use should be addressed in specific situations because they (1) vary widely in their applications and (2) are under legal challenge and are subject to change.

Before proceeding further, I will state that alcohol is considered to be an addictive substance and, in fact, has more addicts than any other substance. The difference between drugs and alcohol is that the use of alcohol is legal and, except where laws define misconduct while under the influence of alcohol, being an alcoholic is not illegal. However, the misuse of controlled substances (either prescription medications or illegal drugs) is against the law. While being a drug addict is usually viewed as a sickness rather than a crime, there is a legal and social difference between the use of drugs and the use of alcohol. This has resulted in differing views by employers and society in general as reflected by the attitudes of employers and in the laws.

Generally, employers do not want to hire people who are actively addicted to drugs or alcohol. I don't blame them, and I am in favor of excluding people who, as a result of their misuse of any substance, might injure themselves, their co-workers, the public, or an employer's property. I believe an employer should have the right to exclude such persons from employment until they have been treated and are no longer an active danger. Most laws support this view, but the view is not universal.

As for drug addicts or alcoholics who have been rehabilitated, I believe that they have a right to secure a job without being discriminated against in the process. I believe they also have a right to privacy in these matters and should not be subject to prejudicial treatment because of their illnesses. Fortunately, the law is generally in agreement. However, the laws vary, and you should find out which laws are pertinent in your state.

Cigarette Smokers

Society and governments have taken generous views concerning the treatment and disposition of drug addicts and alcoholics in the workplace. In the case of those who have been treated and cured, they have been especially generous.

Unfortunately, cigarette, cigar, and pipe smokers have fallen on hard times. Medical studies have declared that being in the proximity of a smoker is dangerous to health, and antismoking campaigns have resulted in laws that forbid smoking in the workplace. Add to this the fact that smokers annually cost employers over $4,000 each in missed work due to sickness. It is not unusual to find employers who refuse to hire smokers at all. They cite as their reason existing laws forbidding smoking in work spaces and the additional cost they add to company-sponsored health insurance plans.

Smokers, with the support of tobacco companies, have spoken out concerning their rights, and there will no doubt be legal challenges. Nevertheless, smokers can expect to be squeezed and discriminated against legally.

If you smoke, my advice is to quit. I know that smoking is a powerful addiction and quitting may be extremely difficult. The fact is that you may be rejected for jobs because of smoking. It may not be fair, but it is legal. Some people view smoking as not only unhealthy but offensive. Nonsmokers outnumber smokers, and being a militant smoker will not gain you any friends. It certainly will not help you advance your career. On the other hand, by quitting you will remove this unpleasant objection and most likely improve your health and add years to your life.

AIDS Victims

Acquired immune deficiency syndrome (AIDS) is a serious medical problem, and that's how it should be considered.

Unfortunately, the social and economic considerations have tended to overshadow other considerations and have made it a major issue in the workplace.

The U.S. Supreme Court ruled in 1987 that people with diseases are handicapped in the same way as defined in the Rehabilitation Act of 1973. While the case concerned a school teacher named Gene Arline, who was fired because of a recurrence of tuberculosis, this decision is cited in cases involving other contagious diseases as well.[1]

AIDS may become an issue under the following three conditions: (1) hiring and testing for hiring; (2) firing because of AIDS or testing positive for the HIV virus; or (3) protection of other workers or customers who come in contact with persons with AIDS. Most state laws protect against discrimination against people who have cancer. Since AIDS involves forms of cancer, it is likely to fall under such protection.

Hiring discrimination occurs when you are asked questions about your physical condition that go beyond your ability to perform your job satisfactorily or violate state or federal laws. For example, if you are cured of cancer (usually defined as total remission of the disease for five years with no reoccurrence), you are protected by the law in most states. If you have a heart condition but can satisfactorily perform the physical requirements of a job, you are protected.

In the case of AIDS, the same protections generally apply, but there are social and psychological aspects that make the disease more frightening to most people. The disease has been determined to be transmitted solely through exchanges of blood and bodily fluids. There is no greater chance of catching it on most jobs than through normal day-to-day social contact. While the disease is 100 percent fatal, the statistics are that seven times more people die each year in the United States from influenza than have died from AIDS since the discovery of the disease. More than 1,000 people die each day from smoking-related diseases, but these do not cause nearly the panic and fear that AIDS does. Perhaps what

---

[1] Darien McWhirter, *Your Rights at Work* (New York: Wiley, 1989), p. 121.

is needed is to have balance and reason applied to job situations where all physical conditions are concerned.

DISCRIMINATION ISSUES IN THE EMPLOYMENT INTERVIEW

There are two stages of the hiring process when you should be alert to the possibility of encountering legal discrimination. These are the employment application and the employment interview.

Before embarking on a list of discriminatory and possibly illegal questions and issues that you might confront, a few words of reason are in order. First, understand that most employers who ask discriminatory or illegal questions probably do so out of ignorance. They ask because of a genuine curiosity, not because of a desire to injure you. Second, even when you encounter an employer with a bias or outright bigotry, how you respond will have an effect on the employer's attitude toward you. Each situation that is discussed has a recommended response. Telling an interviewer that a question is illegal is threatening and won't advance your career goals. Third, a militant attitude or a chip on your shoulder will not help you get a job. Several years ago I interviewed a young black man who had held nine jobs in just under two years. I inquired as to why he had moved from job to job so often. He replied that in each case the employer had racially discriminated against him. I asked him why he was seeking to leave his current job, and he stated the same reason. I then pointed out to him that his current employer was a black-owned insurance company with mostly black employees. He then glared at me and said, "You're just like the rest of them!" At each job he expected to find discrimination, and his attitude ensured that he would not be disappointed.

As diverse as the United States is, it is likely that each of us falls into some minority group. It is just as likely that someone will have a dislike for that group. While this may be illegal and morally wrong, my experience is that most jobs are granted on the basis of individual characteristics—personal or professional. This is especially true in technical areas, where technical knowledge and skills are the driving requirements and are frequently in short supply. My advice is to approach every potential job situation with a positive attitude. Go into every interview with an "I'm going to get this job" mindset, and the results will be equally positive.

The following are examples of some situations and questions you may encounter.

1. *"How old are you?" "What is your date of birth?"* Age discrimination against persons over 40 years of age is prohibited by the Age Discrimination in Employment Act and most state laws.

Recommended Response. If you're less than 40, tell your age. There are no legal bars to discriminating against you and probably little bias. If you are over 40, a recommended answer might be, "I'm old enough to perform all aspects of this job satisfactorily and my experience will give you more than what you're asking for. I can do the job." The employer will generally back off. Persisting in a discriminatory and improper question could result in legal action if you don't get the job. Be sure your body language and manner are low key and nonthreatening when you give your answer. You might consider practicing possible answers to sensitive questions before a mirror, a video camera, or someone who can give you critical feedback.

2. *"Do you have children?"* If this question is asked of a man, it is probably small talk or an attempt at a more intimate or friendly approach. If asked of a woman, it may imply that the woman might assume the traditional role of mother at home in favor of the job. If the woman is asked about the children's ages, the implication is that school-age children could make demands on the mother's time that would interfere with her work. A question such as "Do you plan to have children?" conveys the feeling that a woman may get pregnant and either quit or go on maternity leave. The basis of such questions is a concern about tardiness and/or absenteeism. A proper form of expressing these concerns would be to ask whether the employee is available for work during certain hours. This is legitimate and is a fair question that would be asked of any employee.

Asking "How many children do you have?" may be discriminatory because some religions and ethnic groups tend toward larger families. The only issue that an employer can legitimately be concerned with is whether or not an employee will be at work. Probing into personal matters in order to discover possible areas of concern is inappropriate. Questions about family that fall into this class are almost always directed at women—usually by male employers (although women have been known to have similar attitudes). Whether you have no children or a hundred makes no difference as long as you fulfill your work obligation to your employer.

Recommended Responses. If you are asked about your family, consider the context of the question. It may be friendly conversation or a nosy probe. In the case of the latter, reply "Thank you for asking. My family is very much in tune with my working situation." If asked about your plans to have a family, simply say "My plans are to work and devote myself to my job." Turn each of these questions into a positive, pro-job answer.

In a few instances, the employer will press for a specific answer. In these cases a harder-line answer may do the trick. Try something like "That information is probably more appropriate on a personnel form. Does this mean I'm hired?" In sales, this would be known as the *assumptive close.* Convey your answer with an enthusiastic smile. You don't want to send a message of sarcasm. Rather, you want to transmit that you're enthusiastic and ready to start work.

3. *"Can you work on Saturday or Sunday?"* This is a legitimate question. Whether you can work on particular days is a question that would be asked of all candidates. On the other hand, asking "Would your religious beliefs prevent you from working on any particular days or holidays?" is illegal and potentially discriminatory. Again, the key to a proper question is not the information the employer is seeking, but how he or she goes about asking for it. Asking in a religious frame of reference could be construed to mean that if the candidate were a member of a faith that did not work on certain days, the candidate would be excluded, which would be discriminatory.

Recommended Response. If asked the "Can you work . . . " question in a religious context, reply "I am available any day except . . . " or "I'm not available on . . . ." Make no references to your religion. You can also state whether you have a preference; for example, "I'm available to work weekdays, but not weekends." If you are denied the job, then further investigation may reveal a bias. The problem is that even if you suspect discrimination, it's difficult to prove. The employer would likely say that you were eliminated for some "safe" reason such as a lack of qualifications.

4. *"Have you ever been arrested?"* Because an arrest does not indicate whether there was a conviction or not, such a question is improper. Statistically, minorities experience a greater percentage of arrests. If this question were used as a screening device, it would impact minorities to a greater extent.

Recommended Response. If asked this question, say "I've never been convicted of a felony" or "I was convicted of . . . " and tell your story. If you have a conviction, be prepared to address it. Don't lie or you'll risk the chance of discovery and probable termination. Above all, don't start telling about arrests and making excuses about "being innocent." Always keep unpleasant issues brief and be prepared with a factual, plausible, and acceptable reply.

Dealing with unpleasant inquiries is a communications skill you must master. Not every question you are asked in an interview will necessarily be to your liking. Becoming defensive or refusing to answer will not gain you a thing; belittling or trying to make the issue appear as unimportant will appear unbelievable. The most effective approach is to ask the interviewer what he or she would like to know.

You're not required to strip your soul to answer any question, but you want to satisfy the interviewer without putting yourself in jeopardy. Answer the question to the extent the interviewer indicated when you asked what he wanted to know, and stop. If the interviewer appears to be focusing on the issue, stop answering questions and ask, "Is there a problem?" or say, "You seem to be very concerned about . . . ; perhaps it would be useful if we cleared the air about the matter." If the interviewer is going to reject you because of a problem, you might as well get it out in the open and take your chances.

5. *"Are you a United States citizen?"* This is a legal and proper question. In order to work in the United States, you must be a citizen or have a visa that permits you to work. However, asking the question, "What country are you from?" or "What is your citizenship?" is illegal and improper. Discriminating on the basis of national origin is illegal. If you have a right to work in the United States, you should not be prevented from doing so because of an employer's bias.

Other ways an interviewer might pose an illegal question is to ask whether English is your native language. Asking what other languages you speak is acceptable, but asking the question in such a way that it might be interpreted as discriminating against your national or ethnic origin is improper. Commenting on your accent falls into the same category.

Requesting that you fill out an I-9 form, which is a statement of citizenship status for the Immigration and Naturalization Service is *not* discriminatory. It is a legal requirement, and refusing to fill it out and sign it is sufficient reason for an employer to refuse to hire you. Knowingly hiring illegal aliens or failing to have properly completed I-9 forms on file can mean serious legal consequences for an employer. The employer will also ask you for proof of citizenship (birth certificate, Social Security card, naturalization certificate, or baptismal certificate). Furnishing fraudulent information or materials as proof of citizenship is a criminal offense and can result in imprisonment or deportation.

Recommended Response. If asked what country you are from, reply "I am a U.S. citizen" or "I have a 'green card' and can legally work in the United States." If you are not a citizen but possess a skill that might cause an employer to be motivated to sponsor you for a legal work permit, say "I'm not a citizen, but I have a skill that would enable you to sponsor me for a work permit."

6. *"Tell me about your credit record."* Questions about your financial status such as "Do you own your home or rent?" could be used to discriminate. Statistically, minorities are more economically disadvantaged than the majority of the population, and therefore these kind of questions are inappropriate. If the job requires a qualification of financial responsibility because of business necessity, then it is probably lawful. However, questions that do not relate to the job under consideration are improper.

Recommended Responses. Answer the question with a question. Ask, "Is financial information required for this position?" Or you can respond, "If this job requires a bond or a financial background investigation, I'll be pleased to provide you with whatever information you wish. Do you have a form for your request?" If the question is just idle conversation, the interviewer will most likely drop the subject. Always respond in a cooperative and professional manner.

7. *"Tell me about your physical appearance."* This request is usually made during a telephone interview or on an employment application. It is usually more specific; for example, "color of hair," "height," "weight," or "color of eyes." The answers to these questions can be used to discern race or ethnic origin and are therefore illegal. An exception is if the job requires a particular physical appearance (an actor for example), but it is unlikely that a technical position would qualify.

Recommended Response. Rather than refuse to answer, ask for specifics. Say, "I'm not sure what you're looking for. If you could give me some information as to why my physical description is needed, I'll be able to tell you exactly what you would like to know." There may be a legitimate reason for asking what is an illegal question. It may also be that the employer is asking the question out of ignorance, with no malice intended. Responding in a hostile manner will not help you get a job. Perhaps you may have the opportunity to educate a future employer and prevent a company from unintentionally violating someone else's rights.

8. *"Are you married?"* This question has nothing to do with the job. It is idle conversation at best, and if you are of the opposite sex of the interviewer, it could be a prelude to sexual harassment. Such questions are usually directed at women. They may be more subtle, such as "Are you a Miss, Mrs., or Ms.?" or "What is your prior married name?" These questions are appropriately asked and answered *after* you are hired. Asking about your spouse's work or his or her name is just another oblique way of inquiring about your marital status.

I have heard male employers express concern over women employees. It is based on real or perceived concerns about single women getting married and leaving or married women getting pregnant and leaving. Asking about marital status will not make any difference, but some employers continue to ask questions.

Recommended Response. Look the employer in the eye and ask, "What does my marital status have to do with the requirements of the job?" This is one you don't have to answer and shouldn't. You might ask it in a softer manner by saying, "I'll be glad to provide that information on your employee's personnel form."

PROTECTING YOUR TECHNICAL CREATIONS

Technical professionals face a special issue not normally encountered by their nontechnical counterparts. If they create, design, develop, or invent something, the question arises as to who it belongs to. Is it the technical professional's? After all, it was his or her skills that fashioned the creation. Shouldn't the creator reap the rewards? But what if the person was working for a company that furnished the technical environment and paid the employee for working on the activity that produced the item in question. What happens to the rewards and benefits that occur after the employee leaves that company? What about the inventions that the technical professional might bring to a job? If a company gains some benefit from these inventions, does it owe the inventor something beyond a salary?

These are issues that must be settled *before* you go to work. Depending on the other party to do the right thing will bring you disappointment. The best advice I can give you is to raise the issues prior to accepting a job and then get the advice of a good lawyer.

Inventions and Copyrights

There are several conditions under which an employee might come in conflict with an employer over the rights to an invention.

1. If the employee is hired to develop a product, the product belongs to the employer.

2. If a contract was executed that stated that any products developed by the employee while in the service of the employer belong to the employer, the employee has no claim to the work.

3. If no contract exists, but the employee developed a product on company time, the company has what is called a "shop right" to the invention, which means that the company can use the product without obligation to the employee. The invention, however, belongs to the employee.

The bottom line in any of these circumstances is that if there is any possibility of a conflict over a creation a lawyer should be consulted.

NONCOMPETE AGREEMENTS

It is not unusual for employees in technical markets to be requested or required to sign agreements that they will not compete with their employers after their employment is terminated. The only condition that would reasonably warrant such an agreement is in a case in which the employee is dealing with the employer's customer. Technical professionals involved in development and other technical endeavors will normally not be affected unless they are in sales or marketing.

The major issue driving these agreements is concern over sales representatives taking their customers to a competitor. Noncompete agreements are usually stated in terms of a time period (a year would not be unusual) and/or a geographical area. Noncompete agreements worded in such a way as to forbid a former employee from ever working for a competing organization are difficult to enforce. People—especially technical people with specialized training—have a right to work in their profession.

A greater concern to employers of technical professionals is their going to work for a competitor and applying the technology and skills learned at the employer's expense. Trade secret laws effectively prevent a former employee from transferring technology to a new employer in such a way as to injure the former employer through the loss of a competitive advantage. There is sometimes a fine line between working in your area of technical expertise and violating a trade secret agreement or law. You should be careful if you find yourself being offered a position by an employer who seeks to hire you for the product knowledge you've gained at another company. Even though they might state that they will assume any liability, you should seek the advice of a lawyer. Involvement in an infringement lawsuit will most certainly cause damage to your reputation even though you may be an innocent party. The reputation of a technical professional is more valuable than a chance at a questionable short-term gain.

IF YOUR RIGHTS AS AN EMPLOYEE ARE VIOLATED

As an employee, you have many rights. You have the right to be paid for work you do, the right to work without fear of being wrongfully discharged, and the right to legal redress if the rights you have under the law are violated.

The Fair Labor Standards Act of 1938 controls the number of hours that employees who are paid on an hourly basis can work in a week without being paid overtime. The law also covers other areas such as minimum wage and child labor (which is unlikely to apply to technical people).

The various states also have laws that set forth when wages must be paid. These pertain to how often you must be paid (e.g., weekly, biweekly) and how soon you must be paid if you quit or are terminated. For a more detailed discussion of the applicable laws, including a summary of the various state laws, I refer you to Darien McWhirter's excellent book, *Your Rights At Work.*

Should You Take Legal Action?

A decision to take legal action is serious—particularly where your career and livelihood are concerned. If it does become necessary to litigate, you stand a good chance of prevailing. In a subscription solicitation in October, 1990, the *California Employment Law Letter* stated that a 1989 study by the Bureau of National Affairs revealed that the average jury award to employees who won wrongful discharge cases against employers between 1986 and 1988 was $603,302. It also stated that employees won nearly two-thirds of their cases against employers.

This solicitation was for a publication that informs employers of employment issues so that they can avoid situations in which employees' rights might be violated. The fact is that a majority of employers are ignorant where laws pertaining to employees' rights are concerned, and they are therefore vulnerable.

Whether or not you should take advantage of this vulnerability depends on the seriousness of the violation. Going to court is a stressful experience, and if you can resolve the problem any other way, I would advise you to do so.

SUMMARY

Understanding and exercising your rights as an employee are important to success in your career. You should take time to learn the laws that apply to you and be prepared to stand up for your rights if you feel you have been wronged. The best approach you can take concerning legal matters is to develop a relationship with a competent attorney and heed his or her advice.

12

FINDING HELP
You're Not Alone

I have been in the search and placement business for over 14 years, and a book on the job search process would not be complete unless I passed along some lessons about effectively using third-party sources—commonly called *head-hunters*, *placement services*, and *employment agencies*. I must admit to having a prejudice, but it is a prejudice tempered by experience and observation of many successful job searches.

There are various types of services available, and they are not all equal in their ability to help job seekers. This is important because careers can be enhanced or damaged by the advice these services give. Knowing how to use these sources effectively in your job search, establish and maintain relationships, and use them to assist in managing and directing your career is a valuable tool. It's also important to understand what types of third-party services are available. There are some that can enhance your job search and give you an edge in the marketplace and others that you should avoid; some that are beneficial and ethical and others whose motives are questionable.

The most important issue in your relationship with any search professional is what you should do to maximize his or her services.

USING SEARCH AND CAREER CONSULTANTS: A PERSPECTIVE

Statistically, approximately 9 percent of jobs are made through search and placement services and employment agencies. By comparison, networking is the number one means of job finding at 75 percent. This doesn't mean you should abandon third-party job help because it is a less prevalent means of finding a job. The job search is not a contest in which you pick the "best" method of winning. What matters is that you find the best job, not how you get there.

There is a story about two hikers who were walking through the woods when they suddenly came upon a very large, angry grizzly bear. The bear reared up on its hind legs to over 13 feet in height. It was snarling and growling and obviously unhappy about the intrusion. One hiker immediately sat down, reached in his backpack, pulled out a pair of running shoes, and started taking off his hiking boots. The other hiker, observing all this, asked, "What do you think you're doing? You're never going to outrun that bear!" The hiker with the shoes looked up and replied, "I don't have to! I just have to outrun you!"

As discussed in Chapter 7, smart job hunters use any and all sources in their search. There is no best way to find a job. Their efforts and methods are judged by the quality of the jobs they get.

ATTITUDES ABOUT SEARCH AND PLACEMENT PROFESSIONALS

Let's clear the air about the attitudes and misconceptions many people have concerning third-party search services. I referred earlier to these people as "headhunters." While this is a commonly used term, it is not considered complimentary by most people in the search industry. In fact, it is viewed as an insult by many. However, this is a mild name compared to others I've heard (and been called). Among them are "flesh peddler," "sleazeball," and "money hungry." Like other professionals, we in the search and placement industry want to be viewed in a favorable way. Also as in any other profession, my industry has its share of unethical practitioners. If you have met up with this type of person, your perception of the search and placement profession is probably jaded. In my own practice, I accept these attitudes in candidates I encounter for the first time and work to change them by demonstrating that dealing with a search professional can be a rewarding experience.

Whatever view you may have, I ask that you remain open and judge each person in the search business individually and on the results that person achieves for you. Judging anyone as part of a group is unfair; it is the basis of prejudice. This extends to companies and jobs as well. Get the facts before you make a decision. Hear the other person's point of view before you decide about that person one way or the other. This is not for the other person's benefit, but for yours. I'm not asking you to do this because it will make you a more intelligent and socially acceptable person. I'm telling you to be selfish to the extent that acting in this manner will be more beneficial to your career in the long run.

As you become acquainted with individuals in the search and placement industry, you will come to recognize that they are individuals with different personalities. You will also learn that unethical behavior is the exception, and, as in any other field of endeavor, one bad operator hurts the reputation of everyone. Industry organizations such as the National Association of Personnel Consultants and their state and local counterparts work hard promoting a positive image for their members. While these groups have little ability to police and discipline individual operators, practitioners who are members do agree to operate by the Code of Ethics that is formally proclaimed by the National Association.

SERVICES AVAILABLE TO THE JOB HUNTER

There are a variety of services available to the job hunter, and it is important that people entering the job market understand the services available to them and what would best suit their needs. Because of the specialized nature of the technical professional's work, focusing on the appropriate services is especially important for this group. The following services are of particular interest to the technical professional:

- Retained search consultants
- Contingency search consultants
- Contingency placement consultants
- Contract services
- Independent consultants

- Project contractors
- Full-time contracting services
- Temporary services
- Career counselors
- Outplacement services

Retained Search Consultants

What They Do

Organizations performing retained search services are contracted by employers to identify and recruit suitable candidates for specific jobs. The retained search firm is paid a fee called a *retainer* for performing the search. This fee is usually one-third of the projected compensation. The fee is paid regardless of whether the search is successful or not. As a point of interest, searches are completed at a rate of about 70 percent.

Relationship to the Technical Candidate

Retained search consultants are called "headhunters" because they approach the candidates. This is important to know, because people looking for jobs often contact retained search consultants or send them résumés in hopes that they will represent them to employers. I have heard candidates express bitterness about retained search consultants because they felt they were rebuffed or ignored. The two key points in understanding retained search firms is that (1) the employer is paying and therefore that is who they work for; and (2) they are searching for people with specific, defined skills and abilities. They do not market candidates to employers.

Retained search organizations are also referred to as *executive search firms* because, more often than not, the target of their search is someone on the upper management or executive level. Retained search is seldom used for mid-level positions and never for low-level positions. Highly specialized technical professionals are also often sought out by retained search consultants because of the scarcity and difficulty of and critical need for their skills.

The question for technical professionals is whether they should consider retained search firms a viable resource and, if so, how they can make use of such services for maximum effectiveness.

Since retained search consultants operate by locating and recruiting suitable candidates, the candidate's concern is how to attract the consultant's attention.

What Not to Do

Knowing how *not* to approach a retained search organization is as important as knowing the correct way to be noticed. Calling and trying to get a search consultant to represent you is definitely not the way to get off to a good start in building a positive relationship with that person. My business is primarily contingency search (defined below), which operates in a manner similar to that of retained search firms. Each day I receive several résumés and calls from job seekers. They want my help in finding a job and want me to represent them to my employer clients. When I explain that I search out qualified candidates based on criteria provided by my clients, more often than not I am told how qualified they are and that they should either be represented to my clients or marketed to other companies I might know. The people who really annoy me are the ones who say that they can learn and I should represent them to my clients on that basis. I can appreciate the frustrations of the job seeker, but if I were to represent a candidate to a client on the basis that he or she was a "fast learner," my credibility would be down the drain.

The lesson here is don't ask retained (or contingency) search consultants to market or sell your services to employer clients. That is not their business, and if you press them, you will antagonize them and get nowhere.

How to Get Their Attention

If you have a technical skill, and especially if what you do is unique and on the leading edge of your field, you are in demand. It's highly likely that someone wants to talk with you about employment opportunities. However, using a retained search consultant is not a short-term undertaking. That is, if you are out of work and need a job immediately, working to gain the attention of retained search firms is not the best approach. Retained search is a long-term personal investment in your time that involves promoting and positioning yourself.

Sending a résumé to various search organizations that concentrate in your technical specialty is a good idea. Include a cover letter requesting that you be entered in their data base and stating that, if an opportunity arises that fits one of their client's requirements, you would like to hear about it. This is nonthreatening and lets the firm know who you are without demanding anything from them. They may have something immediately or they may not. In any case, you are not in a hurry.

If you are good in your field, let the world know. Write articles for industry publications and speak at gatherings of other professionals (conventions, symposiums, seminars, etc.). Join professional organizations and network, network, network! To get ahead and be noticed, you must be aggressive and not be shy. Your goal is to have your name mentioned first whenever anyone in your field is asked who is the best.

Contingency Search Consultants

What They Do

A contingency search firm operates in a manner similar to that of the retained search firm. The difference is that the contingency recruiter is paid a fee only if a search is successful. This affects the way the search is conducted in several ways. First, there is an economic incentive for the recruiter to search harder for the right person. Conversely, there may be a reduced incentive because the client is not obligated to pay for services rendered and may change the requirements or terminate the search in midstream. The contingency search recruiter's motivation is usually in direct proportion to the client's past performance. If hires have been made in the past, there is a positive motivation. Finally, motivation may be lessened if the client chooses to release the assignment to a sizable number of contingency search organizations. The theory behind the client's thinking is that the more people looking for a candidate, the better the chances are that the right one will be found. This is a fallacy, because search organizations do not give the same effort to an "open search" as they do to an exclusive assignment. Contingency organizations tend to gravitate toward assignments most likely to result in a hire while putting those with less probability of success on the back burner.

Contingency search organizations tend to deal less with executive and managerial positions than their retained search counterparts and more with mid-level and specialized positions. Since specialization tends to focus on technical fields, this means that contingency placement recruiters are more likely to be searching for technical professionals than top-level executives.

What Not to Do

The same "do nots" apply to approaching a contingency search firm as to retained search firms, but they are somewhat lessened by the fact that many contingency search recruiters specialize in technical fields and may therefore extend a more enthusiastic reception to technical callers than retained recruiters do. If you do receive a favorable reception from a contingency search recruiter, do not call the recruiter back and ask, "What do you have for me?" Be assured that if the recruiter has a potential situation for you, you will be the first to hear. Since *contingency* means that the recruiter doesn't get paid until you go to work, you'll definitely get a call when the recruiter gets an assignment for someone with your qualifications.

How to Get Their Attention

Contingency recruiters want to find you a job because it's the only way they can get paid. If you wish to get their attention you must do three things. First, understand that the contingency search recruiter works from the requirements of employers. This means that if you help the recruiter get assignments from employers, the recruiter will want to help you. If you become aware of a position that the recruiter might be able to work on, pass it along. Better yet, introduce the recruiter to the employer. Even though the job may not fit your qualifications, the recruiter will be in your debt. Second, refer qualified candidates who may be able to fill the recruiter's current needs. This will place the recruiter further in your debt. Third, cooperate with the recruiter when your opportunity comes along. Go on every interview, follow the advice the recruiter gives you, and after every interview you go on— whether it was arranged by the recruiter or not—give the recruiter an update on the position and the company. Helping a recruiter whose business it is to be aware of what is going on in your segment of the job market is a smart career move. When an opportunity that fits your background and abilities presents itself, you will be the candidate who comes to mind.

If you are thinking that helping a recruiter find job openings and candidates to fill them is not a good way for someone who's looking for work to spend his or her time, you are wrong. I have had these types of relationships with candidates and I have placed them, referred them to other search professionals, and provided them with career advice. In addition to mutual business benefits, longstanding friendships have developed.

Contingency Placement Consultants

How They Work

Contingency placement is similar to contingency search in that the employer pays a fee for the recruiter's service following a successful hire. The difference is that the recruiter takes individual candidates and represents them to potential employers. The recruiter calls employers who have technical environments where candidates might work and markets the candidates to their hiring authorities. This is called "running with" the candidate, and the presentation to the employer is called "pitching" the candidate.

How to Get Their Attention

All the ways I've previously mentioned to get the attention of recruiters apply here, plus the following, the most important of all. If you truly want to have recruiters seeking you out, you must ensure that you are "marketable." This means having the background, experience, skills, and availability that the recruiters' clients are looking for.

Unfortunately, the right background, experience, and skills do not come about overnight. They are the result of a career-long effort, and you have to start as early as possible. Picking a marketable career path is a matter of developing skills in a technical area where you will always be in demand. It's also a matter of avoiding dead-end fields where no future jobs are in the offing. You must listen to mentors in your industry who know where the technology is going and follow their advice.

Contract Services

How They Work

Contract services are offered on an hourly basis through a contractor employer or "jobber." The contractor employer identifies qualified personnel, contracts with the client employer for a specific assignment for a predetermined period (e.g., three months to a year or more), then hires the contract personnel to perform the job. If you are the person hired, you are hired on an hourly basis and are paid by the contractor. You work at the client's location but are the employee of the contractor. You may be called a "contractor," a "contract [engineer, programmer, etc.]," or a "consultant."

This form of employment is becoming popular with employers who must staff for project assignments with predetermined completion times. It is especially attractive for technical assignments involving development and implementation requiring highly skilled personnel. It is attractive to employers because the term of employment is for the length of the project only and there is no requirement to add additional permanent staff. This means there are no costs for benefits such as medical insurance, vacation, or retirement. The hourly cost per employee is greater, but this is offset by the savings on benefits and the fact that there is no need to keep the contractor on as a permanent employee.

Advantages of Contracting

There are several attractive features of contract services to the technical professional. The foremost is economic: The money is very good. For example, technical professionals who command an annual salary of $40,000 to $50,000 would probably receive $30 to $50 per hour as contract employees, depending on the demand and how critical their skills are. This translates into an annual income of over $60,000 to $100,000.

Another attractive feature of contracting is flexibility. Contractors work in a variety of locations and environments. They also work with different people at each job site, which gives them a broad professional network. The opportunity to work at many different jobs and tasks gives the contractor a professional and technical perspective that someone who works at a single job for a single employer will not have.

Many contractors claim personal independence as the reason why they work as they do. They enjoy the freedom of moving from job to job and place to place. They like the perception that they are their own boss and can work or not as they choose.

Disadvantages of Contracting

The chief disadvantage of contracting is uncertainty. When you work, the money is excellent. When the contract ends the money ends, and if you do not have another contract money is tight until you find work. If you have set aside money to tide you over during these slack periods, you will probably survive. Another economic disadvantage is that certain so-called "benefits" provided with permanent employment are not benefits but are really necessities. Medical insurance, retirement, sick leave, and vacation are needed for continued personal well-being. A contractor has to provide for these things out of the money paid for contracting. There are no days off with pay to look for another job, and economic hard times can be anticipated if there are long periods between contracts.

Contractors are the first to go if there is a staffing cutback in a company. They are not permanent employees, and there is therefore no obligation to give them severance pay or other benefits. Contractors accept this from the outset, and there is no animosity about being let go.

A contractor is expected to step into a job and be productive immediately. There is seldom an opportunity to learn or get up to speed. Employers do not provide training for contractors. If you are a contractor and you do not perform, your services are terminated and another contractor is brought in. Contractors also do not advance in skills and knowledge on the job. They are paid for what they already know. If contractors wish to receive additional training or add skills, the cost comes out of their pockets.

Contractors do not normally work on the more interesting and creative aspects of a job such as design. They are usually assigned to the routine and mundane tasks that are time consuming so that permanent employees can be freed to work in other (often more interesting) areas.

A serious consideration that a technical professional should be aware of before moving into contracting is that once he or she becomes a contractor, it is difficult to return to being a permanent employee. Employers look with suspicion upon contractors who want to become permanent employees. They hold a stereotype of contractors as being money-oriented. I have even heard contractors referred to as "prostitutes." If you are a contractor and decide to return to a more permanent status, you must be ready with a plausible explanation. Looking for security or looking for a job during economic hard times when there are no contracting jobs is not enough. Employers do not wish to bring an employee on board, provide training, and go through a period of non-productivity while the employee learns the job only to have the employee leave when an attractive contracting job comes along. Acceptable reasons for contractors to return to a permanent position include the desire to build a career, geographic stability, and a sense of security. One contractor returned to permanent employment because in his geographic travels he met a young lady whom he married, and she demanded that he settle down to a permanent job.

Independent Consultants

An independent consultant operates the same way as a contracting service, with the exception that individual contractors do not use middlemen or jobbers. They make their own contracts with the employer client. Whereas with contracting services you would technically be the employee of the contracting service, as an independent consultant you are your own boss.

An advantage of this arrangement is that all monies paid by the employer go directly to the consultant, with no margin or override taken out by the contracting service. This does not necessarily mean that independent consultants will be paid more than they might receive through a contracting service, but it may mean that their services might be more attractive economically than if the employer had to go through a third party.

A major disadvantage is the tax status of independent contractors or consultants. The Internal Revenue Service has set forth stringent requirements that must be met in order to qualify as an independent consultant. Unfortunately, the conditions under which most contractors work do not qualify. The basic premise is that employers are responsible for all taxes, and using independent contractors is viewed as an assumption that taxes are being avoided. If an employer is discovered using contractors when they should be classified as employees, there are severe penalties. For this reason, employers will generally insist that contractors and consultants work through contracting services or operate as employees of the company. Many contractors have established their own companies that serve as contracting services in order to qualify.

Project Contractors

Project contractors bid on long-term projects requiring several technical specialists and management personnel working at different levels on a variety of technical tasks. They become the employer by hiring people with the desired qualifications as full-time employees on salary and benefits. These people work as a team at the client's site until the project is complete.

The advantage to the technical professional is security as a full-time employee. Under these conditions, an individual contractor is less likely to be let go when a project is completed because project contractors usually have several ongoing projects to which the individual might be assigned. There is also an advantage in the experience gained by having the opportunity to work on a variety of projects in a number of different companies without the stigma of being an independent hourly contractor. Project contractors are considered as employees of a single company while gaining a variety of experience. Therefore, to prospective employers, they do not appear to be either job hoppers or someone whose motivation is primarily money.

Full-Time Consulting Services

These are employers who hire full-time technical professionals with specialized skills who can consult with client companies. They include large accounting firms, aerospace companies, banks, and any organization that has clients with needs for technical expertise that they might not be able to fulfill internally. These positions provide excellent opportunities for technical professionals to establish themselves as experts in their field. They have the opportunity to see a variety of companies and gain experience through their consulting duties with these companies. Since the technical professionals are full-time employees, they have job security while being able to gain the experiences and growth normally found only in more independent situations.

Temporary Services

Temporary recruiting services offer low-level support to organizations on what is considered to be a temporary basis. This is usually for a few days or weeks while a full-time employee is absent or until a full-time employee can be hired. These positions are typically clerical, or, if technical, they include jobs such as machine operators or technical writers. Mid-level and high-level technical professionals are unlikely to use temporary services to find jobs.

Career Counselors

Career counselors are not recruitment, search, or placement services. Job seekers pay them a fee for job counseling services. The fee they charge is an indication of what you might get for your money. Conventional recruiting services normally do not charge candidates for their services. My personal belief is that no job hunter should have to pay for finding a job. If a career counselor claims that you will get a job as a result of services provided, that should be what you pay for and only when you have a satisfactory job. Anything less is a misrepresentation.

Career assistance services can be useful in giving training in résumé writing and usage, interviewing skills, interpersonal communication, and career planning. These are valuable skills, and they are worth paying for. However, you should judge the service not by its cost but by what you get for the money you pay. If you acquire a skill or ability that enables you to get a better or higher paying job, the cost is well worth it.

Career counselors often get bad press because of unscrupulous operators. These are usually the result of complaints by dissatisfied customers who feel they were misled as to the services they were supposed to receive. One problem with career counseling services is that they charge a sizable fee at a time when the job seeker is out of work and very likely feeling desperate. These fees can amount to $5,000 or more. Being out of work or feeling that a job change is necessary is very stressful and makes a person vulnerable. To be fair, there are career counselors who are ethical and give good value. My advice is to judge each on his or her individual merits and not tar them all with the same brush.

Many career counseling advertisements imply that the job hunter can expect a high salary by using the services of the career counselor. A typical ad would say something like the following: "Opportunities in the $40,000 to $150,000 range are seldom advertised. This is called the 'Hidden Job Market.' We can help you to tap into this resource. For a free, no-obligation evaluation, call today." Below the ad in tiny type will be words that read something like "This is not an offer of employment. Fee for professional services." This disclaimer allows these people to avoid claims of fraud. However, the person who is considerably poorer and still doesn't have a job will probably disagree.

When I retired from the Marine Corps, I attended a course at the Pentagon offered by Catholic University titled "Strategies of Career Transition." One of the lectures covered the various services offered for job hunters. The lecturer spent nearly half the lecture delivering a strong caveat against using the services of career counselors. He didn't condemn all career counselors, because there are honest practitioners who give value for the clients' investment. He advised the students to do two things to evaluate a career counselor before deciding to use his or her services.

First, he advised getting a statement in writing of the services provided. This should be specific, that is, how many hours of training and consulting are provided, a description of the activities, how many résumés will be sent out, the number of companies that will be contacted on your behalf, and the exact cost of the services broken down by individual activity. As a demonstration, the lecturer called two career consultants and asked them these questions. The description of services given was vague and evasive. When asked about the cost, the reply was waffling and went something like "The cost is dependent on the services provided." When asked what services are provided, the response was "Each program is tailored to the individual's personal needs." It was obvious that this information was not going to be given out. Throughout the conversation, there was an insistence that the caller come in for an "evaluation interview."

Second, he recommended that anyone using such a service ask for references. These references should be randomly selected from an open list, not preselected by the service. You should select ten clients from the previous year and call them. There are success stories to be told, but there are also many unhappy customers. A random selection will give you a feel for who is in the majority and whether you might like to pursue a relationship.

The problem with career counseling services is that their motivation is not in finding their clients high-paying jobs, even though that is what they imply. Their motivation is to recruit clients. After the fee is paid, any service provided is after the fact. If the service is successful in finding jobs for its clients, it has a good selling feature for its services. However, keep in mind that career counselors get their money regardless of whether you find a job.

When I entered the civilian job market, I contacted a career consultant to evaluate their services firsthand. I made an appointment and went to their offices. It was impressive. A beautiful receptionist greeted me in an elegantly decorated entry area. I was asked to sit down and wait. In the 15 minutes before I was called in for my interview, several people passed through the waiting area. They were well dressed and prosperous looking. Upon being ushered into the office of the person with whom I was scheduled to meet, it was apparent that a great deal of effort had gone into impressing me. My interviewer looked like a bank president, and his office was more like a board room in one of the Fortune 100 than an interview room.

I was asked to take a short test, which took less than ten minutes. We chatted about my background for the next 15 minutes, then a secretary returned with my test results. The interviewer looked them over for a minute, then looked up and said, "Your test results are excellent. I believe we can provide a real service for you!" Then he extolled the virtues of his organization and the likely outcome. When I asked him how much it would cost me or attempted to ask the recommended questions, he simply shifted to another subject. Without telling me the cost, he asked me when I would like to begin their program. When I told him I would like to think about it, he responded as if I had just made the worst mistake of my life. It was evident that his job was selling. I had experienced a full court press, a hard sell. If I had not been forewarned, I would not have been able to withstand the sales pitch.

Be warned that these people are experts in overcoming your objections to handing over several thousand dollars or signing a contract. Unless you have researched the service and are certain you wish to consider such a course for your job search, I would not recommend going in for any such "look and see" interviews.

Outplacement Services

An outplacement service assists terminated or laid-off employees in making the transition into the job market. It is a counseling service provided by the employer that helps the employee with résumé preparation, interviewing skills, general job search skills, and mailing services. The outplacement firm performing the service does not guarantee placement of the displaced employee, although it may be directly responsible in some cases. Normally, its sole responsibility is to better equip the employee to find a satisfactory next job.

This is a worthwhile service for both the employee and the company that pays for the service. It is valuable to the employee because it provides professional-level assistance at a traumatic and difficult time. It is valuable to the employer because it puts the employer in a more favorable light as opposed to being viewed as the heavy for making what was likely a difficult economic decision. The company is shown to be caring about human needs. While an outplacement service presents the company in a favorable public image, it is also a real service to both company and employee.

For a person suddenly thrust onto the job market, outplacement can be a tremendous help in terms of real job search assistance and as a psychological boost for the employee's morale. Being able to draw on the services of job search professionals is a valuable resource.

HOW TO WORK BEST WITH THIRD PARTIES

Search firms, employment agencies, and job assistance services are found in large numbers in the job marketplace. They are responsible for a sizeable number of hires and therefore are a powerful resource for the job hunter.

Technical professionals, especially, can benefit from third-party services because the ones most likely to help them are specialists in their technical field. Job hunting is a full-time job, and the job hunter who enters the marketplace every few years is an amateur at the business. Since most of the third-party assistance available is paid for by the hiring employer and is free to the job candidate, using these services is a win-win proposition for the job seeker.

Using Third-Party Resources

There are several things you can do to maximize the effect of the third-party resource.

1. *Never assume the services are not worthwhile just because they're free.* There is a tendency to value only those things we pay a price for. You won't pay money to most search consultants, but you will have certain obligations. Lying back and asking "What can you do for me?" will not help you get the most out of what they have to offer. The first thing you must do is approach the service as a valuable resource and communicate that feeling.

2. *Develop a relationship.* It's easier to help someone you like than someone you don't. This usually takes time, so unless there is an immediate chemistry, expect to invest some time in the relationship. I have candidates I meet and talk with on a regular basis. These are friends with whom I have developed a relationship over the years, and I have stopped regarding them as job seekers. Even as I write this, a friend of over 15 years is in the process of accepting a position as a sales manager through my efforts. Knowing his capabilities and desires enabled me to locate a position where he will be happy and productive. It doesn't always take 15 years to develop a relationship, but it takes an effort on both sides. Most friendships take work, but they're well worth it.

3. *Don't be a pest.* When you contact a search professional seeking help, don't begin calling on a daily or weekly basis to ask "What are you doing for me?" The only way a search firm makes a living is by finding the right people for their employer clients. If they have a suitable position for you, you can be certain you will be called. Even though the response may be friendly, you are taking up time that the search professional could be using to talk to employers— possibly about you.

4. *Keep the search professional informed.* This is not a contradiction to the "Don't be a pest" advice. It is keeping the search professional informed as to your job status, interviews, salary increases, job openings at your current job, and persons who might be candidate referrals.

5. *When the search professional arranges an interview for you, don't pass judgment on the job before you have the opportunity to see what it is all about.* If you turn down job interviews, don't expect to have another chance. Good job opportunities are scarce, and the last thing search and placement recruiters want is a finicky and uncooperative candidate.

6. *If you do want to call the recruiter for a progress check, be creative.* Update your search progress or give the recruiter a possible job lead. Try and do something for the recruiter. Make the relationship a two-way street.

7. *If you come across a piece of information about your technical industry, clip it out and send it to the recruiter.* Attach a note to it saying that you thought it might be interesting. Don't call. You're simply keeping in touch.

8. *If there is a job opening at your current place of employment, suggest the services of your recruiter friend.* Look after other people and they will look out for you.

9. *If you find a recruiter with whom you have a good rapport, be loyal.* When I am called by a job hunter, one of the first questions I ask is "What have you done on your own?" When the reply is "I've sent out 200 résumés and called 15 or 20 search firms," it's very disappointing. They may as well add, "and I'm calling you hoping for a miracle!" After they have blanketed the area with résumés and called every recruiter in town, my chances of being any help are practically nil.

If you decide to use the services of a recruiter, it is best to give one that you respect and trust an opportunity to perform. If you do use more than one, limit yourself to no more than two or three. Allow them a few weeks to search for you before sending résumés directly to employers.

Several job hunters have told me they haven't done anything on their own, but when I began to call employers on their behalf I was informed that their résumés had already been received. This presents two problems. First, it puts an instant damper on my enthusiasm for assisting the candidate in any further job search efforts. Second, the effect of sending a résumé is to block any progress I might be able to make on the candidate's behalf with an employer. A résumé has a high probability of being passed over, while a direct dialogue by a professional recruiter on your behalf to a hiring authority is likely to generate a face-to-face interview.

SUMMARY

The job search is not a task you want to approach alone. In addition to support from family, friends, and business associates, there is much help available from third-party sources. These include retained and contingency search and placement consultants and outplacement services. These services are generally free to the job seeker and are paid for by employers.

Career counselors are persons who assist the job seeker in résumé preparation and distribution, interviewing techniques, and general guidance. Because they are paid by the job seeker, they should be evaluated thoroughly as to services provided, reputation (check references), and service guarantees.

The greatest success comes from developing a strong personal relationship with a few third-party professionals. Don't muddy the water by contacting a large number of them and expecting them to be enthusiastic about you. A maximum of three is recommended.

An alternative to permanent employment is contracting or consulting. The advantages are hourly rates that are dramatically higher (up to twice the equivalent salary at a permanent job), flexibility in experience and exposure to different working environments, and a sense of personal independence that comes from working on your own. Disadvantages include uncertainty and insecurity, since the work is normally short-term; lack of benefits such as vacation pay and medical and disability insurance normally provided by a permanent employer; jobs that have fewer challenges and satisfactions; and difficulty in moving back into permanent employment.

Third-party recruiters are a resource that can add a professional dimension to your job search and give you help not available anywhere else. Cultivate friendly relationships with search and placement recruiters so they'll be there when you need them.

13

A VIEW FROM THE OTHER SIDE

How Employers View Candidates

A job search is a sales activity. You are trying to sell your skills and abilities to a prospective employer. If you labor under the mistaken idea that you can get the best jobs by merely being competent, either you have not been on the job market long or you have chosen to ignore the obvious. In order to get hired, you must meet the expectations of the employer. If your background does this, you are in business. If not, you will be rejected regardless of your competence.

In every sales venture, listening to what the customer (employer) says is important is crucial to a successful sale. With this in mind we will focus in this chapter on what employers have stated is important to them in hiring technical employees. What they have to say may surprise you. Most of them are not interested in a laundry list of skills but in the character and motivation of the candidate.

A HIRING MANAGER SPEAKS OUT

Ken Whitaker, former Vice President of Research and Development for Software Publishers, of Mountain View, California, has some specific concerns about the people he hires. In a speech to the California Association of Personnel Consultants in 1989[1] Mr. Whitaker said that many software engineers and developers were too inflexible in their acceptance of job assignments.

Dealing with Change

According to Mr. Whitaker,

> Software people generally have trouble dealing with change. They go to work on a specific project and not for a company. If the project they were hired to work on gets canceled or delayed, they are frustrated when they are assigned to another project in the company. They must realize the economic necessities that drive company decisions and be a team player.

Before considering a job with a new company, you should understand where the company is going technically. Are they state of the art and on the leading edge of their industry, or are they in the business of manufacturing and maintaining existing technology? Many technical professionals prefer manufacturing and maintenance, while others view themselves as working in advancing technologies. A candidate would be at fault if he or she did not consider company objectives and philosophy along with the job. A hard and fast principle is that workers conform to company objectives. Companies are not responsible for the career paths of their employees. You will hear of companies that talk of "career pathing" and profess to have great concern about the future of their technical professionals. You must recognize that while these expresssions of concern are real, they

---

[1] Ken Whitaker, Speech at 1989 Annual Convention of California Association of Personnel Consultants, San Francisco.

operate within the boundaries of the companies' goals and objectives.

Maintaining Technical Marketability

Professionals should watch what the trends are in their field. When they work for a company, they often do not watch what is going on in their industry and what the trends are. It's hard for professionals to know what the trends are and what they should specialize in. They often get themselves boxed into a stale technology.

As a recruiter, I have seen this happen on countless résumés and in interviews. Software specialists become buried in long-term projects that are either old technology or so specialized that only their current employers can use it. When they go into the job market, their skills and background are of limited marketability. They argue that their skills are transferable and they are quick learners. The tragedy is that, even though they are right, it's hard to sell the idea to a prospective employer.

Mr. Whitaker recommends making known to both current and prospective employers what your interests are and that you want to work in areas of new development. He cites the example of a person who has spent five years working with the UNIX operating system but has developed graphic skills on a home computer and would like an opportunity in that area. His point is well taken. Don't expect employers to come to you and ask you what you would like to do. You must express your interests. It may be that the prospective employer doesn't have opportunities in your areas of interest, and in that case, you may have to look elsewhere. My position on changing areas of interest (or careers) is to use the skills and talents that you have to get on board, but make sure that opportunities exist in your real areas of interest.

Is it deceitful to take a job in one area but have an interest in another? Not at all. You will only be deceiving *yourself* if you think an employer will not expect you to perform well in the job you were hired for. In fact, this is a way you can be considered favorably for other opportunities. I call this method of job changing "bridging," because you are using your current skills to get you a job in a company where an opportunity exists to do what you would really like to do. Bridging into something you like is acceptable, but understand that you will have to pay your dues in the job you were hired for.

No Advertising Doesn't Mean No Hiring

Mr. Whitaker found that his company's advertising attracted more recruiters and employment agencies than bona fide candidates. This was not their intention. Because they were not reaching their intended audience, they reduced their advertising. They still had jobs, but they had more luck recruiting through professional recruiters and networking than through advertising.

Good managers will be glad to hear from you if you are looking for a new and more challenging position. Even if they haven't any positions in your field, they will be pleased to discuss plans and trends for the future, and they can become a part of your network. (See Chapter 7.) High-quality candidates for technical positions are not always available when a company is ready to hire, and a smart manager will maintain a file of people who call for future reference.

Know What Is Profitable in Your Field

Mr. Whitaker's area is microcomputers. If a person wanted to enter that industry as a designer, developer, or manufacturer, there are a variety of choices that can be made. Mr. Whitaker broke it down into hardware and software, and this model can be applied to any technical industry. Hardware represents a costly manufacturing process in an extremely competitive marketplace with a low profit margin (5 to 10 percent before taxes). Software is development-intensive, with low production costs that show a pretax profit margin of 25 to 30 percent. Software has more room for growth and risk taking and more opportunity for creative professionals.

Similar opportunities exist in other technical fields. Don't let yourself become myopic about your profession. Position yourself in the part of your industry that is growing and profitable, because that is where job opportunities are going to be. Flexibility is the key! Read industry publications, talk to people in other segments of your industry, participate in professional organizations, and take seminars and courses in your area. Find out where the demand is, and focus and prepare yourself for that segment of the market. There are usually many areas where growth is found, so don't worry if one or two areas are not attractive to you.

HOW EMPLOYERS VIEW MONEY ISSUES

There is a saying in the search business that "today's employer is tomorrow's candidate—and vice versa!" People who hire are also employees in their organizations and also find themselves in the job market from time to time. As they approach the different roles, it is interesting to observe their attitudes toward different aspects of employment. Regarding money, there are wide differences between the views generally held by employers and those held by employees and job seekers.

A favorite survey topic is to ask employees what is important to them and then have them rank their responses in order of importance. The same survey is conducted with employers, and they are asked to list what issues and areas they feel are most important to employees. The results are revealing.

In every survey, employees and job hunters will list "money" and "salary" in the fourth, fifth, or sixth position. I have even seen it listed last in a list of ten. Self-esteem issues such as "job satisfaction" and "recognition" are almost universally considered ahead of money. Employers, on the other hand, will nearly always place "money" first on their list of what they feel is important to employees. When they are asked how they feel about money in their role as an employee, they will put it far down the list, but they consider that the people who work for them are motivated primarily by money.

This is a lesson in perspectives and points of view. The more valid point of view is expressed by the employees, because they are expressing their own feelings. Employers are only stating how they think someone else feels about a subject.

This generally held attitude can be used to the job seeker's advantage. The belief is usually expressed in a negative context and with a disdain for people who are motivated primarily by money. Because employers believe this to be the case, they are usually pleasantly surprised to learn that the job opportunity, and not the money, is a candidate's foremost interest.

It should be stated emphatically at this point that money is important. It pays the bills and provides a desirable standard of living. However, money isn't the driving issue. You want a satisfying job in which you are productive and feel appreciated. You also want to be compensated fairly with as much money as possible. This is a worthy goal and the employer can identify with it.

WHAT TURNS EMPLOYERS ON

Sharp, well-dressed, professional-looking candidates with an outgoing manner and a positive outlook who give the impression that they can do the job are what employers most frequently claim to be looking for. If you think this sounds too corny, consider the opposite and put yourself in the place of the employer. Would you hire someone who was sloppy or overly casual about dress? Would you hire someone who was so introverted that you believed his or her vocabulary consisted of only "yes" or "no?" How about someone you weren't sure could do the job? Remember that employers have been on the job market many times themselves. Put yourself in their places and reflect on what you would want to see in a candidate like yourself.

WHAT TURNS EMPLOYERS OFF

Sloppy, unprofessional-appearing people who fail to project the ability to do the job turn employers off. Again, put yourself in the shoes of the employer. If you have ever been in a hiring position, you know what caused you to reject candidates.

Too often candidates make rationalizations for why they were not hired. Minority candidates may feel the employer was prejudiced because of race, nationality, or gender, and in some instances this may be partially true. In the arena of technical positions, it is less likely, because qualified and skilled technical candidates are too hard to find to reject them for reasons of prejudice. It is also illegal. This doesn't mean it isn't done, but it is less likely in a technical environment.

Personal appearance is vastly understated as a factor in candidate rejection. John T. Molloy's *The New Dress for Success* (Warner, 1988) is more than a book; it is a formula for personal success. Job candidates who go to interviews with the attitude that how they look and what they wear is unimportant compared to what they know and can do are only kidding themselves.

For the record, knowledge and ability are (or at least should be) the primary factors in candidate competence and selectability. However, a poor appearance conveys a message to an employer that perhaps the candidate doesn't care what the employer thinks, or a statement of independence may be construed that spells future trouble. Whether this impression is right or wrong, a business-like appearance and good grooming will never be misinterpreted. Why take the risk?

A worse situation is to have the skills to do the job but be unable to project that competence. This is a lack of basic communication skills. I know a professor of mathematics at a large engineering school who has probably driven more students out of his discipline than he has taught. He is a monotonous speaker who describes himself as "a man of few words." A man of *no* words would be a better description. He depends on his students' reading the text and working the exercises rather than teaching them and charging them with enthusiasm. His brilliance as a mathematician is overshadowed by his failure as a teacher. If it were not for the tenure system, he would have been put out of teaching long ago.

THE "PEOPLE-LIKE-ME" PHENOMENON

To state that people tend to gravitate toward people like themselves is probably not an earth-shaking revelation. However, to acknowledge that people who hire are biased in their hiring practices will likely conjure up visions of the author's being properly tarred and feathered by the advocates of equal employment and affirmative action.

Unfair as it might be, the truth is that regardless of what the law says or what hypocritical mouthings you hear, people will continue to act like human beings in their dealings with each other. In the technical world there is less bias than elsewhere, but people will still react and hire from their first impressions.

People *do* tend to prefer people like themselves. They may bend over backwards in their efforts to hire without prejudice or to eliminate discriminatory practices, but it is still a fact. A quick walk through a working environment can be revealing. You will see a mix of people, but a sizable number will be of the same race and gender as the manager. If you talk to the group, you will find that attitudes and philosophies are also similar.

This is not a criticism; it is an observation. I'm not even sure the practice is wrong. Even where there is a mix of races and genders, there will be compatible personalities. Hiring people who are similar is healthy if it doesn't break the law or keep qualified people from finding work.

I'm mentioning this phenomenon because technical professionals should be aware of it when they interview. They should understand that the better they match the personality of the person who is hiring, the better the chances are that they will get the job. This means listening for clues in the manager's questions and comments or making inquiries prior to the interview. This can be done either by a third-party search consultant or by contacting people you know who work for the company.

SUMMARY

The best salespeople know that if they are to make the sale they must know what the customer wants. A job search is a sales situation, and if candidates want to "sell" their candidacy to prospective employers, they must identify those wants. This identification of wants is vital to success in any interpersonal relationship. If you've ever found yourself in a sales setting and the sales representative tried to push merchandise at you that you didn't want, you know the feeling. I enjoy stopping at neighborhood garage sales on weekends and perhaps picking up a bargain or two. I'm not looking for anything in particular, but I gravitate to books and records. As I glance over the merchandise, often the person running the sale will see me looking at an item and jump in and start pushing it at me. With me, this is a big mistake. I don't like someone telling me what I want or trying to push something on me that I don't need. To me it's a turnoff.

The same principle applies in any other interpersonal environment. People like to hear what they're interested in and what they want. They block out what they don't currently need or want. The key is to focus on those things the other person wants. For a job seeker, this means finding out what the employer wants and concentrating on those areas.

14

SUMMING UP

Taking That First Step on the Technical Job Search

The advice I have given you in this book works! It goes beyond good ideas or perhaps's and maybe's. I have given you more than just advice on writing résumés or a few interviewing techniques. I have attempted to give you a philosophy of the job search as well as the ways and means of arriving at your goal.

As a technical professional, you will probably always find yourself in demand. If you have the proper education, training, and experience, it's likely the jobs will come hunting for you. If you are satisfied with allowing circumstances or someone else to make the choices that will direct your life, throw this book away, or better yet, pass it along to someone who wants to direct his or her own life.

THE STEPS TO CAREER SUCCESS

You are a technical professional in a society that places a high premium on your abilities. You are a national treasure.

Without you, the technological and industrial might of our country will stagnate and falter. Does that make you feel good? I hope it gives you a bit of a boost. The belief that you are the best at what you are will do more than training and ability to put you on the track to success. If you have education and skills in addition to belief in yourself, there is nothing that can stop you from succeeding.

The next step is to take action concerning your career. First, take stock of where you are now. Where do you want to be a year from now? Five years? Ten years? As a beginning exercise, prepare (or update) your F-A-B. Place your old résumés, letters of commendation, diplomas, and certificates in a file folder. Don't be modest about your accomplishments. You can edit and eliminate material later, but for now include everything.

Second, make a list of your accomplishments, skills, and abilities. Consider the areas where these could be put to use. This is a hard-copy (paper) inventory of what you are and what you can do, with the added dimension of considering other career paths within the scope of your technical skills. For example, you might find that you are qualified for technical sales, training, or technical management. What's important about this exercise is that you match what you *want* to do with what you *can* do. Also, now is the time to assess what you might need in the way of knowledge and skills to realize your ambitions.

Next, with a goal (or goals) in mind, list the intermediate steps that will take you where you want to go. It may be that you wish to continue doing what you are currently doing, but in a different geographic location or company. The planning process is the same. Writing down your goals and the steps to get there will give you a point of reference from which you can measure your progress.

This is the "target" step. Prepare your "paperware" (see Chapter 4) and focus on your target or main goal. As you prepare your F-A-B, cover letters, broadcast letters, follow-up letters, and networking letters, ask yourself whether they are consistent with where you are trying to go.

Now do it! Start making your contacts, scheduling interviews, tracking your follow-up, and going after your goal. The message here is to *take action*. You can read books on career advice and get a thousand points of view. You can hope, plan, and think about what you want to do with your life, but until you take the first step toward that goal, it's only wishful thinking.

PRESENT A PROPER IMAGE

A major emphasis of this book has been to convey the message that a technical professional should present a favorable personal image. This goes beyond clean and neat. It means grooming and dressing in a way that conveys the message that you are professional, businesslike, competent, and the person for the job. The following true story will illustrate this better than any urging I might do.

The Man in the "Electric Suit"

Charlie Johnson was a petroleum engineer who had spent most of his 15-year career working in Saudi Arabia and South America. He had a chemical engineering degree from Georgia Tech and excellent references from the four companies for whom he had worked overseas. His résumé was a model right out of the scores of guides that could be bought at any bookstore. It contained the right buzzwords, and it was the type of résumé that employment managers ate up.

Charlie was the dream candidate. On paper he had all the tickets. He could get interviews simply by answering ads and mailing résumés. The problem was that Charlie couldn't get a job.

I first heard from Charlie when he called my search company after seeing it in a Yellow Pages ad. I must admit that I was excited when he called. After talking about his background for a little over an hour, I began to call my clients immediately. Usually I would schedule a meeting with a candidate that I decided to "market." (*Marketing* is a term used in the search profession when candidates have such a desirable skill mix and are so "marketable" that a significant number of employers can likely use their services.)

In the interest of time, I decided not to meet this candidate. I was concerned that such a hot prospect would find a job either on his own or through another recruiter. Actually, I would have done both him and myself a big favor if I had met with him.

The first company I presented Charlie to fell into line with everyone else who found Charlie desirable—without meeting him. An interview was scheduled, and I was so sure of Charlie's success that I was counting my fee.

About a half an hour after Charlie's scheduled interview time, I received a call from the manager who had expressed interest in Charlie. He said he had granted Charlie a "courtesy interview," which meant he spent a minimum time in order to avoid the impression of outright rejection. He said Charlie came to the interview wearing what he described as an "electric suit." Charlie showed up wearing a green suit, pink shirt, red tie, and a ponytail. While none of this affected his job performance, Charlie's dress was deemed unacceptable for a conservative, image-minded company.

I asked Charlie to come into my office. I wanted to discuss the interview and give him some advice on the importance of personal appearance. Charlie was not receptive. He made it quite clear that his personal tastes were no concern of mine or any employer. They would have to take him as he was or not at all. He pointed out—correctly—that he had held several jobs without any concern over the way he dressed and looked.

The good news for Charlie is that he can probably find employers who will hire him. The lesson he has overlooked is that he may be missing out on some excellent opportunities. Even those employers who overlook Charlie's eccentricities may still have a negative first impression, and that may color the perception they have of him throughout his time on the job.

DON'T SHOOT YOURSELF IN THE FOOT

The greatest threat job hunters face is not from potential employers or from other technical professionals who may be competing for a position. Their greatest threat comes from the damage—intentional or unintentional—that they inflict on themselves. To say that they shoot themselves in the foot is an understatement considering the damage some of them manage to accomplish. An actual shot in the foot will heal and the victim can go on with life. The damage some job seekers inflict on themselves can cripple them throughout their professional careers. The following is another true story about a candidate who damaged her career but probably doesn't even realize it.

Don't Burn Your Bridges While You're Still on Them

Whenever I advise someone on the delicate art of job changing, I offer some timeworn clichés and some clichés that are my own. I tell them about the "wing-walking method of job changing," which means that you don't let go of something that's secure until you have a hold on something else that's equally secure. I also throw in the old but still appropriate advice about not burning your bridges behind you.

The worse case of bridge burning I have ever seen was a chemical engineer named Pam who not only burned her bridges but stood on them while she did it. Pam worked in the adhesive industry. This is a fairly narrow industry with few players. In this type of industry, everybody might not know everybody but it's a small community where somebody will know somebody who will likely know you. Your reputation is a commodity to be guarded.

Pam contacted an outside recruiter who specialized in adhesives, and indicated an interest in leaving her current company. Her reasons for leaving were a lack of opportunity and politics in management. In a small industry, specialists are usually at a premium, and the recruiter did not have to look far to find an opportunity that offered what Pam claimed was missing in her present job. Pam was flown to the prospective employer's location, wined and dined for three days, and introduced to various levels of management, and she left with an assurance that an offer would be forthcoming.

I should interject that before scheduling the interview, which involved a considerable financial commitment by the prospective employer, the recruiter did what in the recruiting business is called a "pre-close." This consists of a thorough brief of the company, the job, and an inquiry regarding the candidate's position on salary. It also involves a direct question that goes something like "If what I said is correct and you find that the opportunity meets your needs, are you prepared to accept a position, and at what salary?"

I know this breaks my rule to job hunters about not answering questions about salary expectations. However, the question is not being asked by the employer, but by the recruiter. It is asked to ensure that the candidate is genuinely interested before advising the employer client to bring the candidate in for an interview. There is no commitment to accept a job, but it is a genuine test of the candidate's level of interest. The recruiter cannot afford to have a client spend a substantial amount of money on interviewing expenses only to have the candidate reject a reasonable offer. This does not preclude the candidate's rejecting the employer because of personal chemistry, position, or an inadequate monetary offer. It is simply a statement of reassurance that the job hunter is truly looking for a change and not just "kicking tires."

Pam was debriefed on her return from the visit with the employer. She indicated enthusiasm about the job and the company and stated that she looked forward to receiving an offer. This information was relayed to the employer by the recruiter, and an offer was made. The offer was attractive. Her current salary was $45,000 per year. The offer was $50,000 plus an incentive bonus of an additional $5,000 after one year. This represented an annual increase to Pam of over 20 percent, which was in excess of the industry average. Pam's reply was that she would think it over. This is not an unreasonable reply, since a job change is a major decision, especially when there is a relocation involved.

What Pam did next was to stand in the middle of her career bridge and throw torches at both ends of it. She went directly to her current manager, informed him of the offer, and used the implied threat of quitting to get him to promise to move her to a project that she felt was more advantageous to her career. When she told the recruiter what she had done, he pointed out the possibility of damage to her reputation in the industry, and she replied by saying, "You've got to look out for your own career; nobody's going to do it for you."

What did Pam do to her reputation? Besides a disappointed and upset prospective employer, there are a number of other areas that Pam should have been concerned about. First, the prospective employer. This particular employer invested over $1,000 in airfare, hotels, and dining, not to mention several hours in interviewing for himself and other managers. The employer may view her as flaky, manipulative, or dishonest. Whatever the perspective, it isn't likely to be complimentary. This employer will probably not consider Pam in the future, and if her name ever comes up in the context of this small, tight industry, it will not be remembered with favor.

Second, the recruiter. Pam, like many candidates, tended to place a low value on the services of the recruiter. After all, the recruiter's services didn't cost Pam anything. The recruiter worked on contingency and was paid by the employer only if the position was successfully filled. Anyway, aren't "headhunters" a sleazy lot who will say or do anything to push a body into a job? So what if the recruiter gets a little miffed? He'll get over it.

Recruiters in specialty industries are even more sensitive about candidates' reputations than the employers. They do not want to present a candidate with a bad reputation because of the effect it has on their own reputation and future business with an employer. By using the recruiter's services to leverage her ambitions at her current company, not only did Pam alienate him, but in a small industry where there are only a few good recruiters, the word is going to get around.

Third, her current employer. At this point, Pam believes she has strengthened her position with her current employer. Actually, quite the opposite is true. While her manager acceded to her demands, he did so under the threat that she would take the other job. Pam's act was a form of blackmail, and it will not be overlooked.

Pam was disloyal. She went looking for another job. She used the specter of leaving a void in the organization to squeeze the manager into doing something he wouldn't have done otherwise. The upshot of the situation is that Pam got her position, but the employer recognizes his vulnerability and will start to prepare for such a contingency should it occur again. This will take the form of starting to look for Pam's replacement. Moreover, although Pam will find herself "in" the group, she will actually be outside where decisions and important issues are concerned. She'll find that she is being "planned around." The trust and confidence that were present before this incident are not there. Instead, there are suspicion and misgiving. Eventually, Pam may be replaced, but it is more likely that she will recognize her situation and leave of her own choosing.

Finally, there is Pam. She has put herself in a bad light in the eyes of a prospective employer, her current employer, and a specialty recruiter. The most valuable commodity people have is their reputation. Pam could have approached the recruiter and discussed her concerns about her job. He would likely have counseled her to confront her manager directly with her concerns and, if nothing was done, proceed with her job search. Instead, she told the recruiter she wanted out. Being truthful is not always easy, but it avoids a world of unpleasant consequences.

Pam will very likely find herself looking for another job in the near future—this time for real. She will carry with her the baggage of what she did on her phony job hunt, and, in a small industry, it will haunt and hurt her. While she thinks she is the winner now, she is the ultimate loser.

BE CAUTIOUS ABOUT COUNTEROFFERS!

Pam is an example of a technical professional who truly believed she was doing the best thing for her career. In her case, the situation was directed by the job hunter, and the people with whom she came in contact were used and manipulated. In many job search situations, the candidate is faced with choices that can be potentially damaging to their reputations and careers. One such situation is that of a counteroffer.

A counteroffer is a response (usually expressed in monetary terms) by a current employer to an offer made to an employee by a prospective employer. The best advice I can give to both the candidate and the current employer is to avoid counteroffer situations. My experience with counteroffers has indicated that in only about one in seven accepted counteroffers does the employee stay on the job for more than six additional months. This is not good for either employer or employee.

Actually, a counteroffer is more favorable to employers because it gives them breathing room to plan for the employee's replacement. Usually, the announcement that an employee plans to leave is a surprise. The employer has made no plans for the replacement of a valuable team member, and, for just a few dollars, the problem is postponed until something can be done about it.

In a counteroffer, the employee is the real loser, for a number of reasons. First, counteroffers are nearly always expressed in dollars. They seldom address the real reason why the employee was looking elsewhere. While money is certainly important, most people will state that they want to leave a company either because they are no longer challenged by the job or because there is some interpersonal conflict with the boss. The money is actually a distraction. It temporarily disguises the true reasons why the employee wants to find a new opportunity, but the real problem remains and it will surface again.

Second, the employee's loyalty is now questionable. After all, didn't the employee look elsewhere and even go so far as to consider an offer? The person is not likely to be trusted regardless of what the current employer might say.

Third, the employee used the other company's offer to get more money. While the employee didn't use a gun, the employer is still likely to view it as a form of holdup. Even if the employee did not intend to leverage the current employer, that perception is there.

Fourth, a counteroffer is a boost to the employee's ego: The employee is told that he or she is indispensable. Frequently, a high-ranking executive delivers and reinforces the counteroffer. This is flattering. There is no anger, only positive words, and after all, who would want to leave and hurt friends? Unfortunately, the employee is often left disillusioned when the reality sinks in and he or she realizes that the nonmonetary dissatisfiers are still present.

Prospective employers are at a disadvantage in a counter-offer situation because they are an unknown while the current employer is not. They represent uncertainty while the current employer is well understood. The current job may have problems, but the employee knows what is going on— even if it is bad.

Fifth, an employee who accepts a counteroffer should understand that it is only a temporary situation until a replacement can be found. Of course, this is not what the employer will *say*. There will be promises that whatever it was that caused the employee to look elsewhere will be taken care of, but the employee must realize, when a deal is struck, that things will never be the same again—and they won't be good.

Sixth, because counteroffers are usually made in monetary terms, they do not correct the real cause(s) for the employee's looking elsewhere. Even when money is the reason, it should cause the employee to wonder why it took someone else's job offer to make the employer recognize his or her worth.

Seventh, when promises other than money are made, the situation is the same. The employee is disloyal, and it will be necessary to find a replacement. Sometimes the money is not in the form of a salary increase, but is an early review, a promotion with an accompanying salary increase, or a bonus. However it is colored, it is still a counteroffer.

Finally, the employee should consider the effect acceptance of a counteroffer has on his or her reputation. The prospective employer who made an offer is going to be disappointed at the least, and possibly angry and vindictive. I have heard employers state that they're glad they discovered what kind of a person the candidate was before they came on board. The employee's reputation is tarnished, and a bridge, possibly a valuable one, has been burned.

I hope I have made the point that counteroffers are not recommended. If you decide to go job hunting, don't back out by way of a counteroffer. Your current position is always a valid alternative. You owe it to yourself, your current employer, and prospective employers to be up front and honest in your dealings with them.

BE A "PEOPLE" PERSON

Throughout this book, I have emphasized the importance of interpersonal communication skills. I used to resent outgoing, articulate people who always had the answers. I finally realized that these people didn't always have the answers, they only *seemed* to. My first realization of this was in graduate school. The Marine Corps sent me to graduate school to major in computer systems and management information systems. My first graduate class was called "Real Time Computer Systems Design." About half the students in the class were U. S. government workers employed in the computer field. They were holding dialogues with the instructor as equals and broaching subjects that were foreign to me. My first impression was that I was in with a group of computer geniuses who had left me in the dust the very first day. To say that I was intimidated was an understatement.

My response was to bear down on my studies, take copious notes, and do the best I could. The intimidation by my glib, silver-tongued classmates continued, and I was sure that if grades were given on a curve, I was sunk. When the time came for the midterm, my anxiety was numbing. When the grades were posted, I was shocked to see that I had made the top score in the class. The grade on my first written report was just as surprising: an "A+" with complimentary notations in the page margins.

This experience was an important lesson for me. It taught me that the appearance of knowledge is not as important as knowledge, but that you can put up a great front if you can communicate well. It turned out that the "geniuses" weren't all that knowledgeable after all. If they were so smart, why were they in the same class I was in? What they were able to do that I couldn't was to communicate what they knew in a way that made them appear knowledgeable. They weren't trying to fool anyone; they just had excellent interpersonal skills and used them effectively.

I became determined to match my knowledge with "people" skills, and I have worked hard to do so. I am an active participant in Toastmaster's International, I teach at three colleges, and I speak before groups whenever I have the opportunity. My job as an employment consultant and executive recruiter depends on my interpersonal skills.

The bottom line is that, as a technical professional, you need to be both technically knowledgeable and able to communicate that knowledge effectively. If you are an introverted person, you must consciously put yourself into situations where you will be forced to exercise your interpersonal abilities.

WHAT HAPPENS IF YOU DON'T SUCCEED?

Fear of failure is one of the major reasons why most people don't try to better themselves. Often this fear is on the unconscious level and many other reasons are given for not taking action. This is natural. The sense of mystery and anxiety that surrounds the unknown and what is in our future is a common feeling in all of us. Fear of change is present in every human endeavor. If you have ever tried to introduce a new idea or a change in the way things are done, you have experienced resistance. You may have been the one who said, "We've always done it this way," or perhaps, "It won't work." It is human to want to keep things as they are and not rock the boat.

Refusing to try anything new or venture out on a new path or reach for a dream or goal is one way never to fail. It is also a way never to succeed. But it is important to remember that failure has a positive side in that it shows you which alternatives won't work. You can learn from your mistakes, and when you try again your likelihood of success is much greater. An excessively optimistic view? I don't think so!

GO FOR THE BEST AND SUCCEED

You now have the knowledge and the tools to take your career to its limit and beyond. The fact that you are reading a book such as this says that you have that desire. Now take your desire and make it a reality.

Go for it and good luck!

Selected Bibliography
and Recommended
Reading

BEATTY, RICHARD H. *The Perfect Cover Letter*. New York: Wiley, 1989.

BOLLES, RICHARD NELSON. *What Color Is Your Parachute?* Berkeley, CA: Ten Speed Press, 1990.

BOSTWICK, BURDETTE E. *111 Techniques & Strategies for Getting the Job Interview*. New York: Wiley, 1981.

BRADY, JOHN. *The Craft of Interviewing*. New York: Vintage, 1976.

BYRNE, JOHN A. *The Headhunters*. New York: Macmillan, 1986.

COFFIN, ROYCE A. *The Communicator*. New York: Barnes & Noble, 1975.

COFFIN, ROYCE. *The Negotiator: A Manual for Winners*. New York: Barnes & Noble, 1973.

COLE, KENNETH J. *The Headhunter Strategy: How to Make It Work for You*. New York: Wiley, 1985.

COLLARD, BETSY A. *The High-Tech Career Book*. Los Altos, CA.: Crisp, 1986.

CONSULTANTS NEWS. *The Lexicon of Executive Recruiting*. Fitzwilliam, NH: Author, 1978.

COTHAM, JAMES C. III. *Career Shock*. New York: Donald I. Fine, 1989.

COUGER, J. DANIEL AND ROBERT A. ZAWACKI. *Motivating and Managing Computer Personnel*. New York: Wiley-Interscience, 1980.

DAHL, DAN AND RANDOLPH SYKES. *Charting Your Goals: Personal Life-Goals Planner.* New York: Harper & Row, 1988.

DEMARCO, TOM AND TIMOTHY LISTER. *Peopleware: Productive Projects and Teams.* New York: Dorset House, 1987.

DONALDSON, LES. *Conversational Magic.* West Nyack, NY: Parker, 1981.

DOWNS, CAL W., G. PAUL SMEYAK, AND ERNEST MARTIN. *Professional Interviewing.* New York: Harper & Row, 1980.

DRAKE, JOHN D. *Interviewing for Managers.* New York: Amacom, 1982.

FAST, JULIUS. *The Body Language of Sex, Power, and Aggression.* New York: Jove, 1978.

FEAR, RICHARD A. *The Evaluation Interview.* New York: McGraw-Hill, 1984.

FRANK, MILO O. *How to Get Your Point Across in 30 Seconds or Less.* New York: Simon & Schuster, 1986.

FRENCH, JACK. *Up the EDP Pyramid.* New York: Wiley, 1981.

GENUA, ROBERT L. *The Employer's Guide to Interviewing.* Englewood Cliffs, N.J.: Prentice-Hall, 1979.

GERBERG, ROBERT. *Robert Gerberg's Job Changing System.* Kansas City, MO: Andrews, McMeel, & Parker, 1984.

HAMILTON, CHERYL. *Communicating for Results.* Belmont, CA: Wadsworth, 1990.

HARMON, FREDERICK G. *The Executive Odyssey.* New York: Wiley, 1989.

HAWKINSON, PAUL A. AND JEFFREY G. ALLEN., J.D., C.P.C. *The Placement Strategy Handbook.* Culver City, CA: Search Research, 1985.

HUNSAKER, PHILIP L. and ANTHONY J. ALESSANDRA, *The Art of Managing People.* Englewood Cliffs, N.J.: Prentice-Hall, 1980.

JAMESON, ROBERT J. *The Professional Job Changing System.* Parsippany, N.J.: Performance Dynamics, 1978.

KENNEDY, JAMES H., ED. *The Handbook of Executive Search.* Fitzwilliam, NH: Consultants News, 1974.

KORDA, MICHAEL. *SUCCESS!* NEW YORK: RANDOM HOUSE, 1977.

KUBLER-ROSS, ELISABETH. *On Death and Dying*. New York: Harper & Row, 1973.

LEWIS, ADELE. *The Best Resumes for Scientists and Engineers*. New York: Wiley, 1988.

MAHLER, WALTER R. *How Effective Executives Interview*. Homewood, IL: Dow Jones-Irwin, 1976.

MAINSTREAM ACCESS. *The Data Processing/Information Technology Job Finder*. Englewood Cliffs, N.J.: Prentice-Hall, 1981.

MARTIN, THOMAS L., JR. *Malice in Blunderland*. New York: McGraw-Hill, 1973.

MCWHIRTER, DARIEN. *Your Rights At Work*. New York: Wiley, 1989.

MEDLEY, H. ANTHONY. *Sweaty Palms: The Neglected Art of Being Interviewed*. Belmont, CA: Lifetime Learning, 1978.

MEYER, JOHN L. AND MELVIN W. DONAHO. *Get the Right Person for the Job*. Englewood Cliffs, N.J.: Prentice-Hall, 1979.

MOFFATT, THOMAS L. *Selection Interviewing for Managers*. New York: Harper & Row, 1979.

MOLLOY, JOHN T. *Dress for Success*. New York: Warner, 1975.

MOLLOY, JOHN T. *Live for Success*. New York: Perigord Press, 1981.

MOLLOY, JOHN T. *The New Dress for Success*. New York: Warner, 1988.

MOLLOY, JOHN T. *The Woman's Dress for Success Book*. New York: Warner, 1977.

MOORE, DAVID J. "Companies Adopt Dual Career Information Systems Path." *Information Systems News*, May 16, 1983.

MOORE, DAVID J. *The Employment Dynamics Seminar Workbook*. Laguna Hills, CA: Realtime Associates, 1981.

MOORE, DAVID J. "How to Begin a Career in Data Processing." *Orange County Business Journal*, November 1982.

MOORE, DAVID J. *Leapfrogging the Unicorn: Tips for DP Job Changing*. Laguna Hills, CA: Realtime Associates, 1983.

MOORE, DAVID J. *Recruiting and Hiring the Computer Professional*. New York: Van Nostrand Reinhold, 1987.

NOER, DAVID. *How to Beat the Employment Game*. Berkeley, CA: Ten Speed Press, 1975.

Olson, Richard F. *Managing the Interview*. New York: Wiley, 1980.

Panza, Dr. Ernie. *The Power of Positive Attitudes*. Williamsburg, VA: Virginia Publishers, 1990.

Pettus, Theodore T. *One on One: Win the Interview, Win the Job*. New York: Focus Press, 1979.

Preston, Paul. *Employer's Guide to Hiring and Firing*. Englewood Cliffs, N.J.: Prentice-Hall, 1982.

Quick, Thomas L. *Inspiring People at Work*. New York: Executive Enterprises, 1986.

Roesch, Roberta. *Smart Talk: The Art of Savvy Business Conversation*. New York: Amacom, 1989.

Rust, H. Lee. *Jobsearch*. New York: Amacom, 1991.

Shingleton, Jack. *Which Niche?* Holbrook, MA: Bob Adams, 1989.

Silver, Regina. *The Directory of Technical-Placement Resources*. Los Angeles: Silver Crown, 1988.

Silverman, Melvin. *The Technical Manager's Survival Book*. New York: McGraw-Hill, 1984.

Stanat, Kerby W. with Patrick Reardon. *Job Hunting Secrets and Tactics*. Milwaukee: Westwind Press, 1977.

Stanton, Erwin S. *Successful Personnel Recruiting and Selection*. New York: Amacom, 1977.

Stern, Barrie D. *Skinetics*. Costa Mesa, CA: Author, 1981.

Stewart, Doug. *The Power of People Skills*. New York: Wiley, 1986.

Stidger, Ruthy W. *The Competence Game*. New York: Thomond Press, 1980.

Studner, Peter K. *Super Job Search*. Los Angeles: Jamenair, 1989.

Tarrant, John. *Stalking the Headhunter*. New York: Bantam, 1986.

"The 10 Most Common Interviewing Mistakes" (commentary). *Personnel Journal* (June 1984): 10.

Tepper, Ron. *Power Resumes*. New York: Wiley, 1989.

Townsend, Robert. *Up the Organization*. New York: Knopf, 1970.

Vervalin, Charles H. *Management and the Technical Professional*. Houston: Gulf Publishing, 1981.

WAREHAM, JOHN. *Secrets of a Corporate Headhunter.* New York: Atheneum, 1980.

WILLIAMS, ROGER K. *How to Evaluate, Select, and Work with Executive Recruiters.* Fitzwilliam, NH: Consultants News, 1981.

WORTMAN, LEON A. *Effective Management for Engineers and Scientists.* New York: Wiley, 1981.

YATE, MARTIN. *Hiring the Best.* Holbrook, MA: Bob Adams, 1990.

YATE, MARTIN. *Keeping the Best.* Holbrook, MA: Bob Adams, 1991.

INDEX

Note: Letter *f* after page number indicates that the entry refers to a figure on that page.